ATOMIC WEAPONS AND
EAST-WEST RELATIONS

By the same author

MILITARY AND POLITICAL CONSEQUENCES
OF ATOMIC ENERGY

(Turnstile Press, 1948)

ATOMIC WEAPONS

AND

EAST-WEST RELATIONS

BY

P. M. S. BLACKETT

CAMBRIDGE
AT THE UNIVERSITY PRESS
1956

CAMBRIDGE UNIVERSITY PRESS
Cambridge, New York, Melbourne, Madrid, Cape Town, Singapore,
São Paulo, Delhi, Dubai, Tokyo

Cambridge University Press
The Edinburgh Building, Cambridge CB2 8RU, UK

Published in the United States of America by
Cambridge University Press, New York

www.cambridge.org
Information on this title: www.cambridge.org/9780521141215

First published 1956
This digitally printed version 2010

A catalogue record for this publication is available from the British Library

ISBN 978-0-521-04268-0 Hardback
ISBN 978-0-521-14121-5 Paperback

PREFACE

I WISH to express my deep appreciation of the invitation of the Master and Fellows of Trinity College, Cambridge, to give the Lees Knowles Lectures on Military Science. I chose for my subject what is by far the most important and the most difficult problem confronting military thought and action today: the effect of atomic weapons on war and on the relations between the Eastern and Western groups of powers. The three chapters of this book follow closely the three lectures as given in the spring of 1956.

In the first I have outlined what, at the present time, is being thought, said and written in Western military and political circles about the acute controversy as to the role of atomic weapons in Western military planning.

In the second chapter I have collected together those main published facts about atomic weapons, their carriers, and the defence against them, which seem of chief importance for the understanding of the factual basis of the present controversies.

In the last chapter I have attempted to do two things. I have tried to filter out from the multitudinous events of the past decade those more important subjective factors, both political and personal, which seem to me to have played an essential part in leading to the past and present climate of opinion. Unless these factors are remembered, much in the present remarkable situation must remain inexplicable. Finally, I have sketched very tentatively and in the merest outline what seem to me should be some of the guiding lines of future military policy.

PREFACE

I wish to express my thanks to the Cambridge University Press for arranging so efficiently for the speedy publication of this book; and to my several friends who have read the script and made valuable comments.

LONDON
May 1956

P. M. S. B.

CHAPTER I

ATOMIC WEAPONS AND WESTERN MILITARY POLICY

1

THE ferment in Western military thought today reflects the difficulties and complexities inherent in a transition from a period of Western atomic monopoly to one of atomic parity between East and West. Many of our most cherished military doctrines were formulated before 1949 when the possibility of Soviet atomic attack did not exist. Now that it does, many of these doctrines must clearly be changed. However, the intellectual and practical impediments to doing so are immense. On the one hand, the conceptual difficulties of the subject are severe: arguments and counterarguments are always complex and often subtle; moreover, they often slide into ingenious verbalisms devoid of real content. On the other hand, immense resources in military materials and training have been lavished on the preparation for methods of atomic warfare which are now being subjected to widespread critical analysis.

Seldom, perhaps, in history can it have been more difficult than at present to formulate a defence policy which is both militarily consistent and, at the same time, politically and economically acceptable.

The importance of clear-sightedness in military thought today can hardly be over-emphasized, but the

B

reasons why it is so important are not, I think, quite those often given. It is becoming generally recognized that the danger of an all-out major East-West war breaking out is now quite small. This is certainly due in great part to the possession by both sides of atomic and hydrogen bombs, and consequently of their power of inflicting vast destruction on each other. Moreover, the chance of a small war sliding accidentally into a major one is not very great. Neither of the limited wars in Korea and in Indo-China led to global war. Moreover, this was before the power of hydrogen bombs was widely understood. Now that this is generally known, and that both sides have them, the tendency towards stability is still greater.

The ill effect today of an unsound military policy thus seems to be not so much that of increasing the risk of a major war as of incurring a great waste of national resources and of risking the loss of power and influence in such areas as the Middle East, on which so much of the present prosperity of the West depends.

According to the military thinking of the past decade, if we spend too little of our resources on preparations for all-out strategic atomic war, we risk being overrun by the Soviet Union. On the other hand, it is now clear that if we spend too much, we have little over for conventional arms with which to fight limited wars.

It is not only vital, both to our military safety and to our economic well-being, that Western military policy should be sensible: it is also politically important that it should appear sensible. Moreover, it should if possible appear so not only to our own population but also to the leaders of the hundreds of millions

2

of the non-Western and non-Soviet nations of the world where neutralism is latent or strong, but whose friendship is important for the West, and who may, in Arnold Toynbee's words, 'hold the casting vote in a competition between Russia and the West for world power'.[1] Unwise military strategy and the unwise diplomacy that goes with it can lose the West—some would say have already lost—important assets of good-will and still more tangible assets of bases and economic advantage.

A further reason why it is important that Western defence policy should appear reasonable to the world at large arises from the problem of disarmament and the control of atomic weapons. To get adequate support in U.N.O. for Western proposals involves convincing a large number of uncommitted nations that our proposals are both sensible and timely. They must therefore be intelligible.

In the second chapter I will discuss in some detail atomic weapons themselves and the aircraft and rockets to deliver them, and the efficiency of defence measures against them. For the purpose of the present discussion it is sufficient to base our arguments on the assumption that there is no effective defence at present, nor is there one in sight, against a large-scale and determined atomic attack on cities and centres of population. In relation to strategic air power, offence has now definitely the ascendency over defence; more-over, this applies to both East and West.

This is the situation which is often expressed by the statement that strategic atomic stalemate now exists; or, if it has not already been reached, that it will be soon.

In considering the question of the degree to which

3

the stalemate has already arrived, or how long it will be before it does, it is pertinent to remark that for the purposes of the planning of the British armed forces, and the division of the arms budget between the three Services and the various weapons, it is the future world situation, not the present one, which must be considered.

For weapons take years to design, develop and be issued to the fighting services; moreover, reorganization of the military roles and training of the personnel is also a slow process. Any change, therefore, in the pattern of Western defence planning from that existing at present must be based on the probable strategic position at least several years ahead.

If, therefore, we envisage the planning of the make-up of Western armed forces for the early 1960's, we shall be wise to do so on the basis of the assumption of approximate technological equality in military and atomic matters between the East and the West.

It follows, then, that we are returning slowly to what has been the normal assumption of military planning throughout the centuries: this is to assume that on the average man-for-man or gun-for-gun, the enemy is our equal. In practice this sometimes proves true; sometimes when put to the test of war one finds oneself superior, sometimes inferior.

The traditional way of assessing relative military strength by counting the number of men, guns, tanks, aircraft, ships available to one's own country and to the enemy, implies the assumption, for planning purposes, of technological parity. Both First and Second World Wars were won by the Allies primarily by their superiority in numbers over Germany, certainly not by any overall technological superiority.

2

I will start the detailed discussion of present-day problems by assuming that a strategic atomic stalemate is already in existence, and consequently that all-out total war between East and West is highly unlikely.

However, even if this conclusion is accepted, as I think it should be, all kinds of difficult questions arise which are partly military and partly political in character. How much of our defence budget should we devote to the preparation for strategic atomic bombing in order to keep total war abolished, how much to air defence and how much to conventional forces? One small but immediate problem is the following: what should Britain do about her hydrogen bomb programme? How valid are the reasons given by the Prime Minister for Britain's opposition to the cessation of all test explosions until at least we have made our first test? What ought the British attitude to be if other nations should make a similar demand?

I want to make it clear at the outset that I do not intend to attempt to answer such questions in detail. What I will try to do is to present what seem to be the main facts and arguments which must be taken into account. Any particular practical decision in the field of Defence must inevitably result from a compromise between various conflicting requirements: the actual working out of such practical policies can only be done by professionals with access to all the facts. Here I will attempt only to sketch in the basic background and outline some broad conclusions.

In my view, the main difficulty in formulating a

rational military policy today does not mainly arise because of any great uncertainty as to the immediate physical destructive effects of atomic weapons, or of the more distant effects of radio-active fall out.

It must be remembered, however, that there are still major scientific uncertainties about the world-wide biological effects that might result from atmospheric poisoning due to large-scale use of atomic weapons. For the purposes of the argument of this book, I will make the assumption that these possible biological effects alone are not at present thought in the West to be serious enough to prevent the large-scale use of at least some types of atomic weapons in war. It is possible, however, that further research work may make this assumption untenable.

Considerable uncertainty, of course, surrounds both the problem of delivering atomic weapons to their target, and the converse problem of intercepting and destroying the enemy carriers. However, it will be argued in the next chapter that these uncertainties are neither much greater than is normal in the preparations for war, nor are they probably of decisive importance for planning purposes.

In my view, the main difficulties attending the formulation of an acceptable defence policy reside in uncertainties as to the readiness of the civilian population of nations to take the risk of atomic attack on themselves. Their readiness to take such a risk will depend on their morale, and this will be influenced by their estimation of the issues at stake and of their chance of survival. It will be seen that an essential element of official British defence policy is that Britain should be able to survive such an attack. If this is not so, much of the policy must be changed.

6

Official Western military policy, at any rate until very recently, gave to atomic weapons three essential roles: to act as the Great Deterrent to prevent the outbreak of war; to win by Massive Retaliation such a war if it breaks out, by the destruction of enemy cities; and to be used in a tactical role in a land war to offset the superiority of the enemy in trained fighting men. Western military planning today is essentially based on using atomic weapons in a tactical role: at S.H.A.P.E. tactical atomic weapons have acquired conventional status.

These three roles may have made military sense while the West had a complete, or nearly complete, monopoly of atomic weapons, but they clearly require reconsideration now that the Soviet Union has also a stockpile of atomic weapons.

It is firstly important to note that the third of these three roles, that of tactical support of land forces, is generally believed in the West to be as useful an aid to Western policy as it was in the time of our atomic monopoly. For detailed published military studies[2] make it plausible to assume that the use of tactical atomic weapons by both sides in a land battle tends on balance to favour the defence rather than the offence and so to induce tactical military stalemate on the ground. This is because the great concentrations of troops required for a traditional offensive will have to be avoided—they provide too good an atomic target.

Since much Western military planning has lately been concerned with stopping by inferior manpower a land invasion of Europe from the east, the use of atomic weapons in a tactical role, even though also available to the East, is generally believed to favour the West.

7

It is most important to note that this prediction may prove false, as so many other military predictions have done in the past. It seems possible that a very highly trained and heavily equipped land army might effectively exploit tactical atomic weapons for offensive operations. By means of these weapons a breach might be blasted through an enemy's defence system. Armoured vehicles specially designed to be as immune as possible to blast and heat flash would be sent through the gap. The gamma-flash could only partially be screened off, but such rays do not produce immediate incapacitation; only illness or death much later. If such a military operation were to prove highly successful, then clearly tactical atomic weapons might cease to be an unqualified advantage to the West.

For the present discussion, however, I will make the now normal assumption in the West, that the use of atomic bombs tactically is likely to favour the West rather than the East, so that their use is not directly affected by the rising Soviet stockpile.

On the other hand, plans for the strategic use of atomic bombs against enemy cities and industrial areas, either as a deterrent to all-out war or as a method of winning one, have been greatly affected by the existence of a growing Soviet stockpile of atomic and hydrogen bombs. If, for instance, the Soviet Union is supposed to have made some substantial but local aggression by land forces, then the earlier conception of the use of atomic weapons would lead to strategic atomic attack on the U.S.S.R. itself.

Now, one cannot suppose that the Soviet Union, if some of its cities were destroyed, say, by atomic bombers from European bases, might not reply in kind on the very vulnerable and accessible cities of

Western Europe. With the present level of active air defence, there is no doubt that some atomic and hydrogen bombs would find their target.

Nowhere in Western Europe, however, is there any serious attempt to prepare for the atomic bombing of cities. Neither in Britain, France, Germany nor Italy have any effective Civil Defence preparations been made. A serious attempt to do so would mean extremely elaborate and expensive preparations, including deep shelters, strengthening of existing buildings, emergency transport and evacuation arrangements, accommodation in reception areas in the country, the stockpiling of food, fuel and other goods. And even if all this were done and the resulting social dislocation faced, the damage and casualties would be immense.

It is undoubtedly the vulnerability of Western cities to Soviet atomic attack and of Russian cities to Western atomic attack which has led to the conclusion that neither East nor West will risk all-out war.

3

British defence policy as expounded in the last three annual White Papers implies that any massive land aggression would be met by the West with *both tactical and strategical* use of atomic weapons.

The difficulties of implementing this policy are brought prominently into view in a recent article by the military correspondent of *The Times* (13 December 1955) entitled 'Disquiet on the Western Front', in which he discusses the military situation in Europe. After mentioning 'the growing realization that massive retaliation is no longer a one-sided affair', he writes: 'Perhaps the most serious aspect is that N.A.T.O. ground forces between the Baltic and the Alps are at their weakest now, just when nuclear weapons appear to have defeated their object by becoming suicidal.' Then the writer of the article proceeds to set out exceedingly clearly the possible reactions to this situation.

The possibility of N.A.T.O. relying solely on strategic atomic bombing, keeping only little more than police forces on the Continent, is rejected as impossible to carry out. Such a policy, which gives the weak ground forces the role of a 'trip wire', would involve unleashing full strategic atomic war to stop even a relatively minor aggression. Clearly this would not happen, since, quite apart from the expectation of atomic counter-attack on the West, the punishment would be grossly disproportionate to the crime. Thus an enemy could well make piecemeal aggressions with impunity.

At the other extreme is the reliance wholly on conventional weapons. This is excluded because it leads to the necessity of matching the East man-for-man, which, it is held, would lead to economic bankruptcy.

The intermediate course is to counter aggression by only as much force, including tactical atomic weapons, as is necessary to defeat it. The aim would be not to extract unconditional surrender but simply to force the enemy to abandon his purpose. This is a policy of making the punishment fit the crime, and is often referred to as a policy of Graduated Deterrence.

The Times correspondent argues that since both sides have atomic weapons and the means of delivery, and since their use would mean mutual suicide, an agreement with the East to use only tactical nuclear weapons is possible.

Two powerful advocates of graduated deterrence as a suitable policy for Britain are Captain Liddell Hart and Rear-Admiral Sir Anthony Buzzard. The former, in a letter to *The Times* in August 1955, gives a careful analysis of the role of hydrogen bombs as a deterrent to massive aggression but holds that 'it is far less sure as a deterrent to smaller aggressions or as a check on the risk of an unintentional slide into an all-out war of mutual suicide'. He then continues: 'The fundamental drawback of the present defence policy, based on the hydrogen bomb, is that it tends to become an "all or nothing" weapon. Unlimited war with nuclear weapons is so frightful a prospect as to cause hesitation, delay and feebleness in reacting to any aggression that is not obviously a vital threat.'

After considering the main obvious objections to this plan, Liddell Hart concludes, 'At present we are getting the worst of both worlds. The lack of clarity tends to combine maximum cost with minimum security.'

Admiral Buzzard gives an elaborate and very detailed analysis of the arguments for and against a policy of graduated deterrence, and concludes that such a policy is certainly desirable and probably possible.[3] The arguments for its desirability are strong. For unless such a distinction can be made, the West would be unable to use tactical atomic weapons to fight a limited war for fear that it would develop rapidly into an all-out strategic atomic war, which the West is quite unprepared to fight.

Admiral Buzzard emphasizes strongly the point that the advent of strategic atomic stalemate does not imply a general military stalemate; for the Eastern powers still have a large superiority in land forces, which, it is held, can only be countered by the use by the West of tactical atomic weapons. So the policy of graduated deterrence is essentially directed towards bringing about a tactical stalemate also.

The question of the feasibility of making in peace and maintaining in war valid distinctions between the tactical and strategic use of atomic weapons is very complex and very difficult to answer.

There are essentially three types of distinction which could be made: a distinction between strategic and tactical targets, a distinction between vital and non-vital areas of the world, and a distinction between small atomic bombs and large ones, including hydrogen bombs.

If I understand Admiral Buzzard aright, he considers that some combination of these distinctions could be moulded into a practical guide to action on the part of the West, and that it would be to the Soviet advantage to conform also. However, he considers that the West should not state too explicitly beforehand in just what circumstances we would employ the three categories of force, that is, only conventional weapons, or conventional weapons and tactical atomic weapons, or finally all weapons including strategical atomic weapons. Apparently, the suggestion is that the West should announce *unilaterally* that it intends to limit the use of atomic weapons to the minimum necessary to repel any specific aggression, but that it should not specify in advance just what particular limitations it would put into operation in any particular

12

circumstances. It will be remembered that the article in *The Times* suggested attempting to negotiate with the U.S.S.R. for such a *mutual* agreement, rather than to make a unilateral statement.

In an editorial entitled 'Cities and Bombs', the *Manchester Guardian* writes: ' "Absurd and impracticable" is what orthodox military staffs may say to the proposals by Sir Anthony Buzzard. . . . These proposals are neither absurd nor impracticable—and unless some such policy is adopted, the military will find it increasingly hard to persuade the public that ordinary forces are worth keeping up. . . . Why pay for armies in Europe if any major war is to mean the strategic bombing of cities at once? . . . Why bother with two years' national service and a bill amounting to millions of pounds annually if the armies are incapable of fighting effectively without nuclear weapons, which would bring on strategic bombing?'

Air Marshal Sir John Slessor, in a rejoinder to Admiral Buzzard's suggestions, also argues strongly the importance of preparing for limited wars: 'We must be able and willing in these circumstances to deal with limited aggression by limited means—in other words by land forces with air cover and support. That is an unwelcome idea, particularly in the United States, but it is one we must face if we are to meet our obligations to our smaller and more remote allies. Unwillingness to do that would result in what Vice-President Nixon has called being "nibbled to death".'[4] On the other hand, he does not think that even if the West used tactical atomic weapons to the full, they would enable the West to match the Soviet tactical strength on land in Europe. So he effectively concludes that even if graduated deterrence were a feasible

13

policy it would not be a successful policy, except in non-vital areas. So, in his view, the strategic atomic striking power of the West retains its primary role as the great deterrent to any but quite minor aggression.

Now, it may well be true that Sir John Slessor's view is correct, that even with tactical atomic weapons the West could not match the East on land. However, this by no means leads to the conclusion that it is possible to return to a policy of massive retaliation except as a suicidal last resort. It is a common fallacy to suppose that the demolition of an opponent's argument automatically establishes one's own.

Dr R. Cockburn, a senior scientist of the Ministry of Supply, speaking in his personal capacity to the Royal United Services Institution in November 1955, rejected graduated deterrence as unworkable and introduced another concept, to which he ascribed the greatest importance.[5] This is the concept of 'the tacit bomb line, that is, a line surrounding objectives which are vital, and clearly seen to be vital, to survival'. The theory of stability by power of mutual annihilation holds only for major actions within the tacit bomb line. Thus no major aggression by either side against objectives within the other's bomb line will occur, because if it did, mutual annihilation would follow. But this is not so for attack on objectives outside these lines, where Dr Cockburn envisages limited wars being carried on rather as in the past, but with the addition of the use of tactical atomic weapons. He argues that the use of such tactical atomic weapons outside the tacit bomb line would not be likely to precipitate an all-out war.

Dr Cockburn's doctrine of the tacit bomb line has much in common with the theory of graduated deterrence. Both envisage types of aggression which would be met by limited action with the limited objective of stopping the aggression rather than totally defeating the aggressor. Both assume that there are some types of aggression which would be so perilous to all that the West stands for that it would have to be met by all-out war, even though this meant the destruction of the West. The main difference in the doctrines seems to lie in Cockburn's emphasis on the geographical distinction between vital and non-vital areas of the world, rather than on a distinction of target or weapon size.

It is clear, however, that the concept of vital and non-vital areas of the world is likely to introduce profound international difficulties. Vital to whom? In Sir John Slessor's and Dr Cockburn's views it is clear that for Western strategy Europe would be a vital area and most of Asia a non-vital area. The former writes: 'If we had to fight in, say, Asian conditions, however, we should have to use atomic weapons to help offset the inevitable numerical superiority of the enemy—the tactical atomic weapon, not the fission-fusion-fission bomb. And it is in these conditions that we might apply some form of graduated or limited use of weapons.'

Now, no one who has had any contact with uncommitted Asian opinion can have any doubts as to the reaction in Asia if the third atomic bomb to be used in war were to be dropped by white men on coloured, as were the first two. No more effective method for adding to the enemies of the West could be devised than by introducing a geographical distinction which might be held in Asia to be a form of atomic weapon colour bar.

15

In general, and in spite of these difficulties and doubts, one may conclude that both the doctrines of graduated deterrence and that of the tacit bomb line, though still incomplete and tentative, are serious and useful initial steps towards working out a rational military policy to replace that of massive retaliation.

Some of the criticisms of the policy of graduated deterrence can hardly be called useful or serious. An article in the *Economist* of 5 November 1955 is worth quoting as an example of misleading verbal precision. After pointing out the obvious difficulties of working out in detail any practical policy of limited war, the author clinches his conclusion that a policy of graduated deterrence is impossible by the statement: 'One reverts to the major premise—if the effectiveness of the deterrent resides precisely in its certainty and its horror, then any attempt to reduce either the certainty or the horror will reduce its power to deter.' This is simple evasion, for the writer must know perfectly well that the circumstances which the proponents of graduated deterrence have in mind are precisely those in which it is *uncertain* whether the West would face the consequences of launching a full strategic atomic attack. Moreover, these are just the circumstances that are likely to occur in the future—as they have already occurred in the past.

Field-Marshal Lord Montgomery upholds eloquently the official British view as found in the Defence White Papers. In a lecture in October 1954 he said: 'I want to make it absolutely clear that we at S.H.A.P.E. are basing all our operational planning on using atomic and thermo-nuclear weapons in our defence.'[6] That he is referring essentially to strategic atomic bombing and not only to tactical bombing is clear from the following passage. 'If we visualize an atomic war, the importance of Civil Defence is apparent. That subject is grossly neglected today. Indeed, there is no sound Civil Defence organization in the national territory of any N.A.T.O. nation so far as I know. . . .Unless the framework of sound Civil Defence organization is set up in peace time, a nation will face disaster in a world war, since the home front will collapse.' Lord Montgomery's reasoning seems to lead to absurdity. Any aggression by land against the West will be met by strategical as well as tactical atomic weapons. This will lead to Soviet attack on Western cities. Since we have no Civil Defence, the Western countries will collapse. Hence his logic leads to the result that any land attack on the West will lead to the defeat of the West.

Then in October 1955, when surely the facts of H-bombs were well understood, Lord Montgomery elaborated again the same general policy. 'The first task of a global war is to win command of the air. . . . Victory in this operation will go to the side that is superior in executing sustained operations in the face of unprecedented destruction.'[7] As recently as April of this year Lord Montgomery again returned to the same theme.[8] Western preparations for maintaining civilian morale in nuclear war were called totally inadequate and far too little attention was being paid to 'nerve and mind war'.

Lord Montgomery is perfectly correct in his view that present Western military policy does envisage action likely in certain circumstances to precipitate enemy atomic attack on Western cities, and, moreover, that no preparations for such attacks are being made.

He does not seem to draw the conclusion that this policy will have to be changed.

Quite different, and much more conservative, views are expressed by General Matthew B. Ridgway, formerly Commander in Korea and later Army Chief of Staff in Washington, in a recent series of articles in the *Saturday Evening Post*.[9] Ridgway argues ably and even vehemently against over-reliance on atomic weapons. He emphasizes that the Soviets were not deterred by atomic bombs when America had an atomic monopoly, and now, when they are drawing level, would be likely not to use them so as to throw the moral odium for their first use on to the West. He thinks that by 1958–62 'Soviet nuclear power will have reached the capability of inflicting critical damage on the U.S. warmaking potential. Soviet air defence measures against our own nuclear bombers will have greatly improved. When that occurs the nuclear-air superiority which the U.S. currently enjoys will have lost most of its present significance.' He then argues for somewhat larger American land forces, very highly-trained, and equipped with air support and air transport, and armed with strong conventional and tactical atomic weapons.

His views imply the existence of a workable distinction between the tactical and strategic use of atomic weapons, and that the former can safely be used without leading to the use of the latter.

Some further very important contributions to this controversy have recently appeared in America. In the January 1956 issue of *Foreign Affairs* Paul H. Nitze, in an article entitled 'Atoms, Strategy and Policy', contrasts the policy of massive retaliation with that of graduated deterrence. He defines the former, in Mr Dulles' words, as a policy of relying for our security 'primarily upon a great capacity to retaliate instantly, by means and at places of our choosing'. The latter policy he outlines as that of attempting to limit wars, in weapons, targets, area and time, to the minimum necessary to deter aggression.

He suggests that the correct policy for the West is as follows. We should attempt to meet aggression and restore the situation without the use of atomic weapons wherever possible. We should only extend hostilities to other areas if there is no other way of restoring the situation. Even if it becomes necessary to engage the U.S.S.R with atomic weapons, we should limit them to military objectives, and initially to those necessary to achieve control of the air, and we should not initiate the bombing of industrial or population centres. Finally, the West should attempt to build up the non-atomic element of its strength, so as to reduce the necessity of reliance on atomic weapons.

Henry A. Kissinger, in an article in April 1956 in the same journal, under the title 'Force and Diplomacy in the Nuclear Age', comments on the fact that President Eisenhower's slogan, 'There is no alternative to peace', is an impractical policy allied to, and in a sense the reverse of, the equally impractical doctrine of massive retaliation. Both are held to be all or none statements inapplicable to the real world we live in. He emphasizes strongly the importance of preparing for limited wars, and so the necessity for the military to develop a doctrine and a capability for the graduated employment of force. The importance of limited objectives is stressed because he holds that 'no power possessing thermo-nuclear weapons is likely to accept unconditional surrender without employing them, and no nation is likely to risk thermo-nuclear destruction except to the extent that it believes its survival to be at stake.'

Kissinger makes the strong point, which has also been made by many others, that, while the power of massive nuclear retaliation may certainly deter aggression, it can also deter defence. The national will-power required to defend one's way of life implies a reasonable chance of survival to pursue it. I consider that these considerations apply with particular force to small exposed countries, and is a very strong factor in strengthening neutralism and may lead to the West losing base facilities.

A particularly powerful contribution to the debate is found in an article by Arnold Wolfers in the Winter 1955/6 issue of the *Yale Review*, entitled 'Could a War in Europe be Limited?' Special stress is laid on the degree to which most people in America till very recently took it for granted that all wars would be fought without restraint or limitation. 'Gone, it was said, was the old distinction between the armed forces and the civilian population, gone the chance of localizing hostilities and of limiting objectives, gone above all the possibility of self-restraint in the choice of weapons or of their targets.' The profound nature of the changes in the pattern of American thought which is involved in the switch from massive retaliation to limited war is emphasized in the remark: 'After all the cost and effort that have gone into the build-up of our Strategic Air Command it may seem preposterous even to raise the question of whether in a war with the Soviet Union it would be militarily rational to initiate the use of this force at all.'

After a very detailed and exceedingly well-argued discussion of the possible advantages and disadvantages of the various methods of limiting war, Mr Wolfers concludes that a war in Europe between the Soviet Union and the N.A.T.O. powers need not become total. Despite the obvious danger 'that any resort to nuclear war may set off a vicious spiral of retaliation ending in total mutual destruction', he considers that 'there is a good chance that atomic attacks in support of land armies in Europe, if carried out with much restraint, would be recognized as such and not set off retaliation on a broader front'.

Mr Wolfers considers that it is just possible that pinpointed attacks on long-range enemy air bases might possibly be consistent with limited war, but that in this case mistakes in target identification might have fatal consequences. The initiation by the West of economy-busting or city-busting attacks is held to constitute an act of sheer national suicide. Finally, he stresses the necessity of limited objectives in war if the enemy is not to be driven as a last resort into precipitating catastrophe for both sides.

These few quotations—one could quote many others with a similar tendency—should be sufficient to show the growing realization of the need for a clarification of Western policy. The specific suggestions discussed above are only some of many possible ones, all of which tend in the direction of returning, except as a last resort, to the more traditional concept of limited war.

Even the concept of 'the last resort' is being subject to critical analysis in America, and serious suggestions are being made that even if strategic bombing of enemy cities had to be resorted to, still it should not be an all-out attack but a city or two should be attacked at a time—so allowing the possibility of negotiation to stop further extension of such bombing.[10]

It is important to note that in most of the arguments for graduated deterrence, particularly in the articles by General Ridgway, Mr Nitze and Mr Kissinger, a strengthening of our conventional armed forces is definitely implied. This would mean lengthened call-up and bigger military budgets.

The most definite statement from official circles, reflecting these views, which I have come across is one by Mr Dulles in December 1955, when he stated:[11] 'We have developed, with our Allies, a collective system of great power which can be flexibly used on whatever scale may be required to make aggression costly'; and that 'our capacity to retaliate . . . would be selective and adapted to the occasion'. This statement suggests that a policy equivalent to graduated deterrence is gradually being adopted in America, even though this is not stated very openly, and even if all the consequences are not being envisaged.

4

Looking as dispassionately as possible at the conflicting arguments, it is hard to understand the present British official military doctrine, with its disinclination to admit openly any restraint on the defensive use of strategic atomic warfare. I have not the slightest doubt myself that both in America and in Britain such restraints are, in fact, already operating. It seems to me certain that the planning going on at S.H.A.P.E. must be based on the assumption that atomic weapons can be used tactically without precipitating their strategic use. For unless this assumption is made, their planning makes nonsense. Can one really believe that S.H.A.P.E. envisage waging a land battle with tactical atomic weapons in Europe when, say, London, Paris, Brussels and the Ruhr cities have been destroyed by atomic bombs in the first week? It is clear that S.H.A.P.E. planning must assume that this will not happen. Now, since active defence will not stop all the atomic bombers, the only way to keep these cities functioning is not to attack similar Soviet targets. So if S.H.A.P.E. is really planning for at least a defensive victory, it must be planning not to initiate strategic atomic bombing. Why, then, is this not openly said by the British and American Governments?

I think the main reason can be found in the complex interaction of military, political and economic factors in America and, to a less extent, in Britain. Much can be learnt from General Ridgway's articles. He states that the American Government's policy (which British policy closely follows), with its extreme emphasis on strategic air atomic warfare, was not an agreed Joint Chiefs of Staff policy. He states that he was deeply shocked when President Eisenhower in his State of the Union message of 1954 said: 'The defence programme recommended for 1955 is based on a new military programme unanimously recommended by the Joint Chiefs of Staff.' General Ridgway, who was one of them, said that he never agreed to this new military policy. He alleges that this programme, with its great emphasis on massive retaliation by strategic atomic air power and its proposals for a reduction of land forces, was forced on the military largely for

23

financial reasons. 'Massive retaliation at the time and place of our choosing' was evidently thought to be cheaper than a balanced defence policy—also more popular politically. It seemed to provide the possibility of both being tough with the U.S.S.R. and of balancing the budget. As so often in the past, strategic air power has been acclaimed as a *cheap* way of exerting military power.

In the British White Paper on Defence, published in February 1956, one finds very little explicit reflection of the widespread doubts and criticisms of the present policy, which are the main subject of this chapter. There is no mention of the vital question of how we can hope to get the assumed advantage in a land war of the tactical use of atomic weapons without precipitating an all-out strategic war which would lead to the destruction of Britain.

To my mind, the discussion of Civil Defence in the White Paper is dangerously inadequate, and full of inconsistencies. For instance, we find the following sober and objective statement:[12] 'To give full protection to everyone from sickness or death from the hazard of radioactivity alone would involve physical preparations on a vast scale, and to make such preparations against all the hazards of a thermo-nuclear attack on this country would place a crippling burden on the national resources. Whatever the preparations made, an attack on this country would involve loss of life and destruction on an unparalleled scale.' Then we find in the following paragraph: 'Nevertheless, within the proportion of our resources that can be made available for home defence, the Government's aim will be to take the precautions without which, should the worst happen, ordered society could not survive.' The con-

cealed assumption is that the funds made available for
Civil Defence, which only amount to some £50 million
a year, are in fact adequate to enable ordered society to
survive an all-out atomic war. This is certainly untrue.
Ten times this sum over several years might possibly,
but not by any means certainly, achieve this objective.
This is one example among others where a flagrant
lack of quantitative thinking has been glossed over by
a suave phrase.

Suppose that the Government were considering
whether or not to launch an atomic attack on Russian
cities as a reply to some local aggression—this is what
British defence policy amounts to. The Government
would then have to consider what would happen if the
U.S.S.R. made an atomic counter-attack on British
cities. Then, I believe that their readiness to launch
such an attack would hardly be any greater than it
would be if we had in fact no Civil Defence at all.
Our existing Civil Defence organization and expendi-
ture has, no doubt, a number of valuable social effects
such as to make individual citizens aware of the
dangers, but as a contribution to making atomic
strategic attack on Russia a possible military reply to
a land aggression I believe it to be effectively non-
existent.

It is often assumed that Britain would launch a
strategic atomic attack automatically and instantly if
large-scale land fighting broke out between East and
West in Europe. I doubt this—at any rate, so long
as the Western land armies were still fighting. For to
do so would most likely cause them to be eventually
defeated by the destruction of the Western cities on
which their supplies depended.

Let us try realistically to envisage the conditions

under which the British Government would itself launch a strategic atomic attack on Russian cities or permit American atomic bombers to do so from British airfields. The only circumstances in which I think they might possibly do so would be *after* but not before one or more British cities had been destroyed by Russia.

After studying carefully the 1956 White Paper and speculating on the omission of all references to the deeply serious controversies exercising students of military affairs, I came to the conclusion that, while our official defence policy may conceivably be intelligent, its presentation in the White Paper is not intelligible.

I believe that the serious inconsistencies in the military policy officially expounded have their origin in a failure of the writer, or writers, to make their military theory match up with their proposed military practice. The final practical recommendations seem perhaps a not unreasonable way of spending the available money: the military theory, however, is not consistent with them.

Much of the general argument of the last two Defence Papers reads much more as if it were intended for the moral and political exhortation of the general public rather than as a serious analysis of strategy for statesmen. No doubt the waging of the Cold War demands much moral and political exhortation; but I think this mixes dangerously with military analysis. For one thing, the statesmen of the vital uncommitted areas of the world will think much of it absurd. We may thereby lose valuable friends—and bases. Perhaps an even greater danger is that the authors will end by believing their own propaganda—to the detriment of their military judgment.

I was somewhat confirmed in this view by the analysis of American policy by Paul H. Nitze in the article already mentioned. He distinguishes America's 'action policy' which he holds is (or at any rate should be) graduated deterrence, from her 'declaratory policy' which is still massive retaliation. The writer then analyses the dangers which arise when the declaratory policy, propounded for its political effects, diverges too far from the action policy on which the military would act.

I think this analysis applies closely to British defence policy at the present time. Failure to distinguish the two aspects, which are both present in the White Paper, is the source of much confusion.

To understand how the gap between British action policy and declaratory policy has come about, it is necessary to remember the important distinction between the various phases of the Western doctrine of massive atomic retaliation. In the first period of Western atomic monopoly, when the U.S.S.R. had no atomic bombs, that is, from 1945 to 1949, Western atomic power was seen as making possible a quick and cheap victory over Russia in the event of a conflict. The manpower superiority of the East was to be met and cancelled out by the technological superiority of the West. In this first period atomic retaliation was assumed to be able to *win* a global war, and so was a surety that war would not break out.

In the second period, from 1949 to about 1953, which may be called the period of quantitative superiority, the growth of Soviet atomic power, though still less than that of the West, made the possibility of a quick and cheap victory over Russia increasingly impracticable.

In the third period which started about 1953 and in which we now are and which for planning purposes can be considered the period of effective atomic parity, strategic atomic attack on enemy cities can only be envisaged as a last resort of a nation driven to the last and suicidal extremity.

The intellectual confusion of British defence policy today is due to a failure to admit fully the transition from the first through the second to the third period. The mainly theoretical parts of the White Paper stem from the first period: the practice is beginning to show signs of reflecting the third, though still very incompletely.

One more quotation from the White Paper is worth giving: 'It is sometimes argued that with the build-up of a stock of nuclear bombs by the Russians, the deterrent value to the Western Powers of building up a stock of bombs and the means of delivery will diminish. This is not so.'[13] This statement asserting that the rise of Soviet atomic power has not made much difference is an extreme simplification. For though it may not have affected the use of atomic weapons as a suicidal last resort, it has certainly greatly diminished the *types* of aggression which can be deterred by Western atomic power,

Moreover, if the above statement were strictly true, why should the West have tried so hard, and be still trying, to maintain at great cost its atomic superiority? As late as 1954, the White Paper asserted that it was essential to keep this superiority.

Even if one admits that there must always be some divergence between action and declaratory military policy, the present gap seems alarmingly wide. It reveals a lag in military and political thought behind facts which is hardly likely to lead to the formulation of a consistent, sensible and intelligible military policy.

We seem to be making just the opposite mistake about air strategy to that we made before the Second World War. Then we grossly *over-estimated* the capabilities of our bombers to deliver their bombs to their targets, and we grossly *under-estimated* the amount of chemical bombing which a civilian population could withstand. Now, if official policy is to be believed, we seem to be equally greatly *under-estimating* the capabilities of enemy bombers and even more *over-estimating* the amount of atomic bombing which the country could stand.

Moreover, it is often the same individuals, who before the Second World War espoused Douhet's theories of military decision by air power alone and later found that civilian morale was much higher than expected, who now as a reaction swing to the other extreme and assume that civilian morale is much tougher than it clearly is.

It may be useful here to comment once more on Mr Dulles' exposition in January 1954 of the doctrine of 'massive retaliation at the time and place of our choosing'. This was not in fact new, for it is essentially the policy of 'instant and condign punishment' of the Baruch Plan of 1946. In 1946 this policy was not possible because America had too few bombs: in 1954 it was not possible because Russia had too many. Perhaps at some intermediate date it might have worked. I will take up this question again in my last chapter.

The announcement was unfortunately timed. Apparently mainly for political and budgetary reasons, a strategic policy belonging to the period of monopoly was disinterred just when even the period of quantitative superiority was drawing to its close. Of course, we see now that this reassertion of the theory of massive retaliation turned out to be, in Mr Nitze's terminology, a declaratory policy. The action policy, as put to the test three months later at Dien Bien Phu, can be described simply—it was inaction. As has been cogently argued by Thomas H. Finletter,[14] no possible better case for the implementation of the policy of massive retaliation at the time and place of our choosing could be imagined than the situation in Indo-China in the spring of 1954. The gap revealed between the two policies became flagrantly revealed to the world at large.

This episode serves as a strong warning against unrealistic military thinking. To explain away the fiasco of Dien Bien Phu, the writers of the so-called 'Brink of War' article in the American magazine *Life* attempted to justify the policy of massive retaliation by alleging that, but for this policy, the defeat would have been still greater.[15] As the Red Queen in *Alice* might have said, 'I could show you a defeat compared with which you'd call that a victory.'

The detailed practical plans for the different arms outlined in the Defence Paper of 1956 may well be the best that can be devised at the present time in the present climate of opinion. However, there is certainly some justice in the criticism that we are trying to have a little of everything and not enough of anything.

The new emphasis on smaller but harder-hitting forces, made highly mobile by air transport, seems soundly adjusted to the increasing importance for planning purposes of local limited wars.

Just in so far as preparations are made for limited local wars, so it becomes increasingly vital to achieve in practice some distinction between tactical and strategic bombing. If this cannot be achieved, then I believe that limited wars will have to be fought without the aid of tactical atomic support. In all likely limited wars, the choice seems to me to be not so much between whether to use atomic bombs strategically as well as tactically, as whether to use them only tactically or not at all.

It is not possible to estimate from the Defence Paper the total national effort going into the preparation for long-range strategic atomic bombing. The atomic weapons budget is not published, nor is the proportion of the air estimates devoted to their carriers. Even if these figures were available, it would be hard to judge whether the amount of effort was reasonable. For one needs for such a judgment an acceptable theory of their use in case of war, and this we certainly have not got. One thing is quite certain. If the theory of their use were actually that given in the White Paper, then the amount spent on atomic weapons, their carriers and on the active and passive defence measures to meet an enemy atomic attack, would be grossly inadequate.

However, I do not think that even the writers of the White Paper take the theory seriously, so probably the practical recommendations are not as absurd as they might at first sight appear.

On the side of the material make-up of our armed forces I want here to make only one comment. Effort put into long-range strategic atomic carriers should clearly be pruned to the limit. For these contribute little to the types of wars and military operations which are likely to happen, in fact, are happening today in various parts of the world such as North Africa, Kenya and Malaya. Nor do these weapons play a useful part in such areas as Korea, Cyprus and the Near East, where land and tactical air forces are needed to maintain a traditional power position.

In point of fact, the existence of Western strategic atomic power and the current official theory of its use, far from strengthening the West's military power position in these areas, probably on balance greatly weakens it. For a small nation, politically sympathetic to the West and traditionally willing to give base facilities for British land and tactical air forces, might well be deterred from giving base facilities for strategic atomic air power, since if global war did break out, destruction would follow.

If it is in fact true, as most current opinion holds, that strategic air power has abolished global war, then an urgent problem for the West is to assess how little effort must be put into it to keep global war abolished.

CHAPTER II

THE ATOMIC ARMS RACE, 1945–55

1

In the first chapter I gave an outline of some of the major problems facing Western military planning now that both America and the Soviet Union have a stockpile of hydrogen bombs and that neither side can envisage an effective defence against them. Much of our present military organization was planned several years ago when the West possessed without any doubt, if not a complete monopoly, at any rate such a qualitative and quantitative superiority in nuclear weapons that the possibility of a serious atomic counter-attack could be neglected. Now, there has never been any room for doubt that the West would have to face, sooner or later, the implications of effective atomic equality provided that one or other of two unlikely events did not occur: that the Soviet Union would disintegrate politically or that either the East or the West provoked a major war.

What has surprised all the Western prophets is the rapidity of the Soviet nuclear development, and of the associated long-range aircraft and ballistic missiles to carry them. Thus the necessity for reorienting military planning concepts has become actual several years before it might have been expected.

As a matter of historical fact it has happened that the advent of atomic parity (for planning purposes) has about coincided in time with the production of hydrogen bombs, and so with the overwhelming advantage of offence over defence. It might have

33   c

happened differently. America might have produced hydrogen bombs before Russia produced atomic bombs; alternatively, Russia might have reached atomic parity before hydrogen bombs were available to either side. In either of these hypothetical cases, the problem of Western military planners would not have been the same as it is today. Now we have to compete with two problems at once: that of the virtual non-existence of a defence against the vast destructive power of hydrogen bombs, and their availability to both sides.

Clearly some very difficult decisions on Western defence policy must soon be taken. I do not myself think that these decisions are greatly affected by the precise figures (even if they were known) of the number of bombs of different types available to both sides in the struggle between East and West, or of their precise destructive power, or of the number and performance of carriers for the bombs, or of the exact capabilities of the various defence systems. However, it is still useful to keep in mind some of the basic numerical facts relevant to the present situation.

It is, of course, conceivable that some of the facts have been kept so secret that no public judgment of military policy can have any great significance; in fact, that the military authorities have up their sleeve some invention or device, the possession of which completely alters the military situation. On reflection we can see that it is fairly safe to disregard this possibility. The basic facts of weapon performance and particularly of atomic bombs, as far as they are known to the military, do eventually, and often quite quickly, become known to the world at large. Aircraft types are openly displayed and approximate performances are freely mentioned, as indeed are also production rates and first-line strengths. Of course, innumerable technical details of weapons, their carriers, new radar equipment, navigational aids, air-to-air and ground-to-air guided missiles, etc., are and will remain secret. In many cases, however, their effectiveness in actual operation is inevitably still unknown to the Armed Services themselves. Often all that the military planners can do is to make approximate estimates of overall performance of a defence system in such a statement as: 'In a large-scale nuclear attack by British nuclear bombers against Soviet cities (or alternatively, by Soviet nuclear bombers against British cities) it can be expected that in average weather conditions at least some given fraction will get through.' During the Second World War, the fraction of bombers which got through was seldom smaller than ninety per cent: only the most optimistic estimates in America put the number as low as twenty per cent for the defence against a Soviet atomic attack on that country. It can be seen that even such a very wide uncertainty as mentioned above, that is, from ninety per cent to twenty per cent, in the chance of a nuclear bomber getting to its target, does not seem likely to affect very greatly the essential military decisions that have to be taken. If none get through, corresponding to perfect defence, matters would be different, but of that there is little likelihood. On the other hand, if all get through, as would happen when inter-continental nuclear armed rockets of adequate accuracy are developed, not much will be changed in the present situation—except perhaps to make clearer what the present situation really is.

I believe therefore that, as regards information at

its disposal, the informed public can be in nearly, if not quite, as good a position as the defence authorities to formulate military policy. It would perhaps be only a slight exaggeration to say that the military planners keep secret from the public only those things which they themselves do not know.

It could hardly be otherwise in our present society. One special reason why this should be so at the present time is that the public itself is the military target of much contemplated military action. In order to instruct it as to what blast damage and injuries, radiation burns, radiation poisoning, and so on, may be coming to it as a result of atomic attack, it has proved essential that almost everything that is known about these things is quickly made public.

Then Members of Parliament, leader writers and military critics must be given enough information to have the possibility of expressing rational views on defence policy. The deliberate concealment or falsification of important defence facts is too dangerous a practice to be maintained.

In the long run, in Western defence matters at any rate, only the truth, even if only approximate, pays.

For consider the case of a Western government which deliberately exaggerated the efficiency of its active defence against air attack. One immediate result might be to reduce the national will to create an adequate Civil Defence, the weakness of which is today one of the most inconsistent aspects of our present official defence policy.

Or suppose a government exaggerated its power of inflicting by atomic attack mortal injury upon the enemy at small cost to itself. Then it becomes politically difficult to explain why important military actions by an enemy against the West have to be allowed to succeed without check: as, for instance, at Dien Bien Phu.

So we can conclude that a careful study of official statements, together with a critical use of unofficial statements, cross-checked and numerically analysed wherever possible, can give any member of the public who makes the effort a reasonably sound factual basis for an independent judgment of military policy.

In considering the material aspect of the use of nuclear weapons there are four main factors in addition to that of Civil Defence, which has already been discussed. These are the bombs themselves, together with the damage and destruction they produce; the bomb-carriers, whether aircraft or rockets; the active defence against enemy nuclear armed carriers; and lastly, certain physical facts of geography relating to target systems, defence perimeters and the location of bases.

2

The fundamental scientific discovery of the nuclear fission of uranium induced by fast neutrons, which is the basis of what are usually called atomic or nuclear bombs or simply A-bombs, was made by Otto Hahn in Berlin in 1938. This was, of course, only the culmination of a great stream of scientific discoveries made in many lands, which created modern nuclear physics. The possibility that a fast chain reaction might be started in a lump of uranium so as to produce an explosion of unprecedented violence soon occurred to many scientists in many countries. With the outbreak of the Second World War in September 1939, serious consideration in England, France and America of the possibility of making a nuclear bomb led to the stopping, at the end of the year, of all publication of scientific results bearing on the subject. The story of the next years has been told too often to need repeating here except in outline.

The first self-sustaining slow nuclear reactor designed by Enrico Fermi in Chicago came into action early in December 1942. In the autumn of 1942 the vast Manhattan project under General Groves was initiated in the highest secrecy and the Los Alamos laboratory was started under the direction of Dr J. Robert Oppenheimer. On 18 July 1945 the first test explosion was made in New Mexico and on 6 and 9 August bombs were dropped on Hiroshima and Nagasaki.

The bomb dropped on Hiroshima was made of Uranium 235, a natural isotope of that metal which was separated from uranium, in which it occurs to the extent of 1 part in 140, by electro-magnetic methods. Later on Uranium 235 was separated by diffusion, which is now the usual method.

The bomb dropped on Nagasaki three days later was made of plutonium, an element which does not exist in nature, but can be made in nuclear piles by the capture of a neutron by Uranium 238.

For both Uranium 235 and plutonium there is a critical mass or size below which they are safe and above which an explosion takes place. This occurs when a fast neutron-induced chain reaction takes place, in which an appreciable fraction of all the heavy nuclei present undergoes fission into lighter nuclei with the emission of a huge amount of energy. One process of producing an explosion consists essentially in very rapidly bringing together pieces of material to form a mass of more than the critical size: this might be done by some form of gun. Details of the actual mechanism used in modern bombs have not been published. It is clear that there are several other possible ways of initiating such explosions. One is the implosion method, in which the uranium or plutonium core is surrounded by a large mass of chemical explosive, which, when exploded, produces such a high pressure that the nuclear core is compressed sufficiently to go over to the critical condition. Another method, perhaps used in conjunction with one of the two methods mentioned, might be to rapidly drive away from the vicinity of the fissile material a lump of some material which inhibits the chain reaction from starting by its property of absorbing fast neutrons without undergoing fission.

The total mass of the fissile material in the early type bombs has not been officially given, but is widely and reasonably held to be about ten pounds. On the other hand, the actual complete weapon with initiating mechanism, as used in the first bombs, has been stated to be some five tons, and also to have been very bulky, so that at that time the large B 29 long-range bomber was the only aircraft able to carry it. Much lighter and less bulky atomic bombs have since been made: some weighing only half a ton and recently atomic bombs have been mentioned in the press as being as small as a teapot—or in another account, as a grapefruit.

Very detailed accounts have been published of the destructive effect of these early type fission bombs. The blast wave from the explosion is similar to that which would be produced by the explosion of 20,000 tons of T.N.T. In addition, there is a very intense burst of heat radiation and of gamma-rays.

The number of people killed at Hiroshima and Nagasaki was 70,000 and 40,000 respectively, with about a similar number injured. Of these, some fifty per cent were by mechanical effects and burns due to fires, twenty-five per cent due to instantaneous burns from the heat flash, and fifteen per cent due to radiation burns from gamma-rays. Of the deaths, ninety per cent occurred at a distance of less than $1\frac{1}{2}$ miles from the point under the explosion, which occurred at a height of 1000 to 2000 feet. The area in which ordinary buildings were nearly completely destroyed was about 6 square miles. About 2000 tons of ordinary chemical bombs would be required to destroy this area. Reinforced concrete buildings survived except in the central square mile or so.

Since 1945 America has produced both rather weaker and much more powerful fission bombs, ranging from one-quarter to some twenty-five times the explosive force of the 1945 bombs, which are now called the standard or nominal fission bomb. Since the radius of destruction varies as the cube root of the explosive power, the area of destruction varies as the two-thirds power of the explosive force, the largest fission bombs, with a T.N.T. equivalent of 500,000 tons will give an area of destruction of some ten times that of a standard bomb, and so about fifty square miles.

The rate of production of bombs in America has not been officially announced, but many plausible estimates have been made by clearly well-informed people based on such figures as numbers and output of plutonium piles, output of diffusion plants, uranium supplies, electricity consumption, etc. By 1955 the American output may have been around a few thousand bombs a year, with the total stockpile of some 30,000 or so of many different types.[1] These would range from large bombs for strategic bombing of big cities, to medium and small bombs and shells for tactical use in land warfare. Other uses of atomic weapons are as anti-aircraft shells and for anti-submarine purposes.

Although British scientists played a decisively important part with their American colleagues in the initial phase of the development of atomic weapons, and continued to play an important role in some of the later scientific developments during the War, the main technological effort which led to the first bombs was overwhelmingly an American one. When Britain started planning her own independent atomic programme in the autumn of 1945, she had to start almost from the beginning as regards the technical 'know how' of pile design and bomb construction. The first British atomic bomb was tested in Australia in 1952, seven years after the explosion of the first American bomb.

There does not seem to be available in the West any reliable published information as to when the Soviet atomic energy programme really started. It cannot be doubted that, if it had not started before 1945, it must have been very energetically pursued after Hiroshima. The first test explosion was made in August 1949, four years later. This is about a year longer than the time which elapsed between Fermi's first pile in 1942 and the first test explosion in 1945. The U.S.S.R. had after 1945, on the one hand, the advantage of knowing definitely that atomic bombs were possible but, on

41

the other, she had a far less developed industry and, moreover, a war-devastated country. The speed of this development work was a surprise to the West, and must have been particularly so to the British atomic authorities, who were not ready for their own first test explosion until 1952.

Various guesses have been made of the present stockpile of Soviet bombs,[2] accumulated since their first test explosion in 1949. A plausible estimate would be a few thousand, say between five and twenty per cent of the American stockpile.

Although much less definite information has been published about the mechanism of a fusion or hydrogen bomb than of a fission bomb, the general scientific principles on which it is based have long been known to all the scientific world. If two very light atomic nuclei, such as hydrogen or lithium, are made to fuse with each other to form a different nuclei, a large amount of energy is emitted. This is the process which goes on in the centre of the sun and which keeps the sun hot and so makes life on earth possible. However, this fusion process requires a very high temperature to initiate it, calculated to be some tens of millions of degrees. The only way known so far of producing such a high temperature is to use the explosion of a powerful A-bomb made from Uranium 235 or plutonium. Thus a fusion bomb in its simplest conceptual form consists of a fission bomb surrounded by a ton or so of some mixture of light elements. When the fission bomb detonates, the temperature of the light elements is raised sufficiently to start the fusion process, and so releases an immense amount of energy—many hundred times that of the fission bomb itself.

The most likely light elements for such a fusion process are the two heavy isotopes of hydrogen, deuterium and tritium, and one or other of the two isotopes of lithium, that is, lithium 6 or lithium 7. Calculations of the rate of emission of heat by various combinations of these at various temperatures have been published in scientific journals as far back as 1950.

Now deuterium, or doubly heavy hydrogen, can be separated from ordinary hydrogen in various ways such as by electrolysis and chemical exchange processes. It is a relatively cheap substance now being sold by America for power-producing piles at a rather low price. On the other hand, tritium, or trebly heavy hydrogen, does not occur at all in nature but has to be made in uranium piles. Since some eighty kilogrammes of plutonium must be sacrificed to make one kilogramme of tritium, the substance must be extremely expensive. Not only is tritium expensive but it is radioactive, so that half of it disappears every twelve years. Moreover, the heat of this radioactive decay has to be removed by cooling plants during storage.

To go from these general principles, which were understood at least as early as 1946, to a practical fusion bomb has proved a very difficult task. By now a large literature exists of scientific calculations and speculations, inspired and uninspired leaks, and official but incomplete statements, from which a plausible but still incomplete picture can be pieced together of the development of the American and, to a lesser extent, of the Soviet hydrogen bombs.

Although consideration was given to the possibility of hydrogen bombs at Los Alamos as far back as

1943, little serious work was done until after the first Soviet fission bomb in 1949.

The first American test explosion of a fusion device took place at Einewetok in November 1952. An official statement gave it an explosive force of some four million tons of T.N.T., that is, two hundred times the explosive power of a standard A-bomb. There is much speculation as to its mechanism. Possibly it consisted of an A-bomb core of plutonium or Uranium 235, surrounded by a mixture of liquified deuterium and tritium, which was itself surrounded by ordinary uranium. It has often been said that this explosion was of a large and cumbersome device, including low temperature plant to liquify the deuterium and tritium, and so was much too large to have been dropped as a bomb. The idea of surrounding the tritium-deuterium charge with a casing of uranium to absorb the fast neutrons produced in the fusion reaction seems to have been one essential step. The uranium itself would then undergo fission and greatly add to the power of the explosion.

A second essential step seems to have been to replace the tritium-deuterium mixture by the solid chemical compound lithium 6-deuteride, that is, a chemical compound of deuterium with the light isotope of lithium. Since little or no tritium is required and since the deuterium is not used in liquid form, this type of dry bomb is much smaller and vastly cheaper than the type using liquid tritium and deuterium.

In August 1953, nine months after the first American fusion test, the Soviet Union exploded a fusion device.

Two more American fusion bombs were tested in March 1954, one or both of which are believed to be fission-fusion-fission or dry three-decker type.

These are believed to consist of a central exploder of plutonium or Uranium 235, surrounded by lithium 6-deuteride with, in addition, a shell of ordinary uranium. The detonation of the fission exploder heats the lithium 6-deuteride to a high enough temperature to cause fusion, and the very fast neutrons emitted in the fusion process are capable of causing fission in the shell of ordinary uranium. The explosive power of such bombs can easily exceed twenty million tons of T.N.T., that is a thousand times that of a standard fission bomb.

Moreover, this type of three-decker fusion bomb is tremendously more deadly than a simple fission-fusion bomb because of the immense amount of radioactive material produced. Whereas a simple hydrogen bomb exploded in the air produces little more radio-activity than the fission bomb which acts as the exploder, the triple type of bomb, which derives most of its energy from the fission of ordinary uranium, may give as much as five hundred times the radioactivity of a standard bomb. This will spread throughout the atmosphere of the globe. It is quite possible that this effect may be serious enough to set a rather low limit to the number of H-bombs which could be used in a military operation without doing serious genetical damage to all the peoples of the world.

When an H-bomb is exploded so low down that the fireball touches the earth, an immense amount of radioactive dust is carried up into the atmosphere and subsequently re-deposited many miles from the explosion, mainly in a down-wind direction. This 'radioactive fall out' can produce a lethal intensity over tens of thousands of square miles. Owing to this, no H- or large A-bomb could ever be exploded low down in a tactical operation against a limited target.

In a comment on a speech by Dr Willard Libby, a member of the Atomic Energy Commission, in June 1955, the *New York Times* declares: 'The significance of this announcement is held to be enormous. To physicists it means that Russia or any other country able to make ordinary atomic bombs can, with a little more effort, create super weapons of the megaton class [megaton = million tons of T.N.T.]. The great complication and expense hitherto associated with the manufacture of the thermo-nuclear bomb becomes negligible.'[3]

During 1955 another large H-bomb has been exploded in the U.S.S.R., which it is reasonable to assume was of the fission-fusion-fission variety, and which is claimed by the U.S.S.R. to have been dropped from an aircraft.

In February 1955 Winston Churchill announced that Britain was developing her own hydrogen bombs, and it has recently been announced that the first test will be in the Pacific in 1957.

If the above account is correct, the qualitative level of the technical development of fusion weapons must be about the same in America and the Soviet Union, with Britain about three years behind. Quantitatively America has without a doubt a much greater stockpile of ordinary fission bombs and possibly also a much greater rate of production. If, however, it is correct to suppose that the U.S.S.R. has a stockpile of a few thousand ordinary bombs (say, ten per cent or more of the American stockpile), and if the reports quoted are correct in asserting that it is a simple and cheap matter to convert a fission bomb into a fission-fusion-fission bomb with a thousand times the power, then one must assume that the Soviet Union could soon have an appreciable number of hydrogen bombs. It is true that America could presumably soon have considerably more. However, the destructive power of these bombs is so large that there are many strategic circumstances in which the side which has, say, a thousand hydrogen bombs is not in an appreciably stronger position than one with, say, two hundred: as it is often put—saturation of strategic atomic power sets in.

Little specific observational data has been released as to the actual destructive effect of hydrogen bombs. However, many detailed estimates have been made by 'scaling up' the effects of atomic bombs. This is done in detail and authoritatively in the recently published *Manual of Civil Defence* issued by the Home Office. Using the scaling method already mentioned, a standard H-bomb of ten million tons of T.N.T. equivalent will have a radius of destruction of twelve miles and so an area of destruction of four hundred square miles. This is rather larger than that of Greater London.

In considering the effect of a strategic bombing campaign waged against a great power, and in attempting to assess the number of bombs of different types which are likely to be required to inflict decisive damage, the following figures are of interest. Let us compare the number of successful aircraft sorties required to destroy an area of four hundred square miles when the three types of bombs are carried. The relative number of sorties are 1 for H-bombs, 50 for A-bombs and 10,000 for chemical bombs carried by bombers with a ten-ton load. These figures are alone sufficient to show why the problem of effective defence against H-bombs is almost insoluble—so few bombers can be permitted to get through.

The number of bombs required to produce a given military effect can be roughly calculated in two ways: by enumerating targets by number and area, and by extrapolating from experience of chemical bombing in the Second World War.

Detailed target studies[4] made in the U.S.A. suggest that some 50 H-bombs or some 300 A-bombs delivered to key targets would knock the U.S.A., at any rate temporarily, out of a war. How many more bombs would have to be dispatched will depend on the fraction of bombers shot down and on the navigational accuracy. A few thousand would be a good guess.

Figures of the same order are obtained by extrapolating from the fact that over one million tons of chemical bombs were dropped on Germany in sixteen months of 1944 and 1945 without, by itself, being decisive.[5] The corresponding number of standard atomic bombs, at 2000 tons of ordinary bombs to one A-bomb, is 500. Remembering the lack of decisiveness of this attack and that the U.S.A. has over twice the population and over fifteen times the area of Germany, one sees again that one would require to dispatch a few thousand standard atomic bombs to inflict decisive injury on the U.S.A.

The corresponding figures for the U.S.S.R. are probably rather larger due to the somewhat greater population and the greater area. For the U.K. perhaps some two hundred atomic bombs dispatched, or perhaps some five to ten hydrogen bombs would suffice to knock her, at least for a time, out of a war, however well prepared with passive and civil defence organization, and however high the morale. Fewer would be needed in the present condition of almost non-existent Civil Defence.

Suppose Britain expected, during the first month, say, of an atomic war, to have launched against her some 1000 sorties of A-bombers. Then to prevent collapse, much fewer than two hundred bombers can be allowed to penetrate the defence: let us take one hundred as the maximum number of A-bombs Britain could take and survive as a fighting unit. This, then, would mean that not more than ten per cent of the attacking A-bombers can be allowed to penetrate the defence, that is, ninety per cent must be shot down. This would be extremely difficult to achieve with our present or our projected defence system. If some of the attacking bombers carried H-bombs—one would not know which—more than ninety-nine per cent would have to be shot down to achieve an effective defence: this is certainly impossible.

3

To wield atomic air power the carriers are as important as the bombs. From 1945 to 1949 America not only had the only atomic bombs in existence but had long-range, rather slow, piston-engined bombers, which could carry the heavy and unwieldy early A-bombs to an operational range of some 1600 miles. The Soviet Union, on the other hand, had paid little attention during the War to long-range bombing and had concentrated its air effort on the design and production of very large numbers of day-fighters, fighter bombers, and specialized ground attack aircraft. All these were operationally linked with the army in land war.

In 1945 the turbo-jet engine had already become operational in fighters both in Germany and Britain but not in long-range bombers. From what we now know, the Soviet Union must have started an energetic programme of jet engine and aircraft development soon after the War. Since in 1945 jet aircraft were relatively new to the West as well as to the East, the Soviet Union did not start very far behind in their development. The first impact on the West of Soviet aeronautical progress since the War was the appearance in Korea of the M.I.G. 15 day-fighter, which seems to have come first into service in 1949. This fighter was rated as aerodynamically at least as good as the American Sabre, and outclassed the British Meteors then operating in Korea. The high kill ratio obtained by the American fighters against the Chinese- and Korean-piloted M.I.G. 15 fighters is attributed to better training and a better gun-sight.

However, it was not until the autumn of 1955 that much publicity was given in the West to Soviet aeronautical progress. One of the first and most detailed of the articles was by Charles J. V. Murphy in the September 1955 issue of *Fortune*, which gave many figures and compared them with those for American aircraft. He also describes the reactions of the American Air Staff to the situation revealed. Apart from subsequent confirmation, one was disposed to consider Mr Murphy as well informed in these matters since it has been officially stated that he has at times acted as spokesman for high Air Force circles, particularly in relation to the H-bomb controversy.

Similar figures are found in the 1955 edition of Jane's, *All the World's Aircraft*, published late last autumn. Then in the first weeks of this year a spate of articles has appeared in the American and world press.

In using the wealth of material revealed in these speeches and articles, one needs to exercise caution, since in some cases motives are undoubtedly present tending towards exaggeration of the Soviet strength. Many of the statements may be influenced by partisanship in inter-service struggles centred on the division of the defence budget. Then the usual grumbles, common to all the three Services, about the inadequacy of the total defence budget, provide motives for over-emphasis of Soviet strength. However, since different groups have different motives, the general conclusions are likely to be reasonably valid.

During March and April 1956, the essential correctness of most of these estimates of Soviet progress have been officially admitted, particularly by Mr Quarles,[6] the United States Air Force Secretary, and by the President himself.[7]

The main striking force of the American Strategic Air Command (S.A.C.) consists at present of some 1500 or so medium-range jet bombers, B 47, though there are still many of the nearly obsolete piston-engined B 36 type. In addition, the first small supplies of very-long-range inter-continental bombers, the B 52, are now coming into service.

The Soviet aircraft corresponding to the B 52 is Type 37, named the Bison in the West. This is reported to weigh 180 tons (a little more than the B 52) and has a maximum speed of 560 m.p.h. and a one-way range of 6000 miles, both said to be somewhat less than the B 52. It has four jet engines each with 15,000 to 20,000 pounds thrust. Some dozen or so of these craft have been seen in the air at once.

Senator Jackson, in a speech in the Senate on 1 February, deems especially ominous the fact that the Soviets seem to be able to design and mass-produce new aircraft quicker than America can.[8] He asserts that the Bison was developed from first design to first production in four years compared with six years for the B 52. The planned production rate for the B 52 was said to be some 12 a month by the end of this year, while the planned production rate of the Soviet Bison was estimated at 25 a month by the end of the year, that is, twice as large. On 4 May, it was stated that 78 American B 52 aircraft have been built compared with an estimated 100 Soviet Bison.

In medium-range bombers, America has a big lead by reason of the 1500 or so B 47 aircraft now in Strategic Air Command. These are the aircraft seen so often by their sky trails over England, and on which the main atomic striking power of the West at present depends.

The production rate of the comparable Soviet medium bombers is the Badger, of which the production rate is said to be 30 a month. This is a 75-ton two-engined jet bomber, somewhat comparable to the British V-class and rather smaller than the B 47. Fifty of these have been seen in formation in the air. The TU 104 passenger jet aircraft recently seen in London appears to be a civil version of the Badger.

The Bear is a very-long-range turbo-propeller 150-ton aircraft which has no Western parallel and which may either be a tanker or bomber. It is credited with a speed of 500 m.p.h. and a one-way range of 8000 miles.

Missiles which, after their initial acceleration by rocket motor, follow a parabolic ballistic trajectory are generally now known as 'ballistic missiles'. The first of these, the war-time German V 2, was a remarkable technical achievement at the time; it weighed 14 tons, carried a 1-ton warhead to a range of 200 miles and with a mean aiming error of some 4 miles. It was accelerated initially by a bi-fuel rocket motor to a velocity of some 5000 feet per second, and then describing a parabolic trajectory, reaching a height of 50 miles.

It has been universally recognized ever since the War that with sufficient technical developmental effort multi-stage ballistic missiles of much longer range could be produced. The artificial satellites round the earth, which are now being planned, are examples of such projects. As military carriers of atomic warheads they have the probable disadvantage of low accuracy at long range, but the advantage of there being no defence in sight against them.

One reason why these missiles have come to play an important role in atomic military planning lies in the now small size and weight of some atomic fission bombs. Now that the required pay load of an atomic missile has become so small, the attainment of long ranges has become easier. It has recently been stated that some new method has been devised in America by which H-bombs can be made small enough to be carried in an inter-continental missile. This seems very unlikely.

It may be interesting to recall Senator Jackson's actual words on the relative ability of the West and the East to deliver atomic bombs: 'Seven years ago, we had a monopoly of atomic bombs and planes for delivering them against distant targets. Today both monopolies are gone. Furthermore, we cannot now even be confident that we are ahead of Moscow in long-range air power.' After showing how America has just kept ahead in the technical race, but with a constantly diminishing margin, the Senator said, 'However, Mr President, I believe that the Soviet Union may win the next critical race for discovery. I believe the Soviets may win the race for the inter-mediate-range 1500-mile ballistic missile.' Such a weapon is often called I.B.M., or intermediate ballistic missile, to contrast it with I.C.B.M., or inter-continental ballistic missile, with a range of some 3000 to 4000 miles. Senator Jackson considers it possible that the Soviets may fire an I.B.M. by the end of this year. Other reports suggest that Soviet missiles of range up to 800 miles may already exist. In April this year, President Eisenhower said that he believed that the American and Russian positions were roughly equal in the race for guided missiles.[7]

Senator Jackson then finally gives a highly-coloured sketch of the disastrous strategical effect of such a Soviet weapon.

4

The main defence system against atomic bombers consists still today of manned fighter planes aided by elaborate radar installations, both for the early tracking of the hostile aircraft and for the guidance of the defending fighters to intercept them. From what has been published, it is likely that as regards quality of modern fighters there can be little to choose between East and West. For instance, the Farmer is a two-jet fighter of the M.I.G. family, with 50° sweepback, which is held to be faster than the American F 100 but slower than the projected Lockheed F 104. Then, the Flashlight is an all-weather and night-fighter somewhat like the Northrop F 94. The combined production of Soviet day- and night-fighters is given as 200 to 300 a month.

It is emphasized, particularly by Mr Murphy, that the Soviet military authorities believe in massive air defence. This is indicated by the 15,000 sub-sonic M.I.G. 15s which have been built and the 8000 M.I.G. 17s which are in service.

Many people, including Senator Jackson, conclude from such figures that the United States is now losing its air atomic lead to the U.S.S.R. and that in three out of four categories of aircraft, that is, long-range jet bombers, day- and night-fighters, the Soviet production is ahead of the United States. Only in medium-range jet bombers has America still the lead.

Little has been reported of the relative position of East and West in relation to guided missiles for defensive purposes. In the West a vast amount of developmental work is in progress, directed towards two main types of weapon: an air-to-air missile to replace the cannon now carried by the fighters and a ground-to-air weapon to replace anti-aircraft guns and eventually fighters themselves. When these are fully developed and widely available, the defence against attacking bombers should be markedly more efficient than at present. However, it does not seem at all likely that any such defence system which, for instance, Britain would be able to build and pay for, would constitute an effective defence against A-bombers and still less against H-bombers.

5

We must now discuss some geographical considerations. The range of the B 47 bombers, on which at present the main striking power of the West depends, is about 1600 miles and so is too small to allow attack on the U.S.S.R. from bases in America. They are thus essentially dependent on the ring of advanced overseas bases. To be sure, operation from the States is possible with two refuellings—once on the outward journey and once on the return. But the tankers also need bases and, moreover, are in short supply. Thus at present the striking power of the S.A.C. depends essentially on its overseas bases. Important among these are those in Greenland, Iceland, Britain, North Africa, Saudi-Arabia, the Philippines, Formosa, Okinawa and Japan.[9]

Assuming these bases can be protected and so kept in operation, then geography is on the side of the United States and against Russia.[10] For Moscow is only 1500 miles from East Anglia, Kiev 1600 miles from Algeria, and Rostov less than 1000 miles from Cyprus. Omsk, in the heart of Central Russia, is 2800 miles from East Anglia. On the other hand, the main S.A.C. bases are deep in the United States and are over 5000 miles from Warsaw and from Murmansk. They are 4000 miles from Anadyr, a remote and big Soviet base near the Behring Straits.

However, all these overseas American bases are within easy striking distance of a 1500-mile missile from existing Soviet bases: consequently if the U.S.S.R. possesses such weapons of adequate accuracy, they could be easily and quickly destroyed. Then the S.A.C. would be forced to retreat 5000 miles to America, and the only striking force left to the S.A.C. would be the long-range jet B 52. After giving these figures and arguments, Senator Jackson said, 'Mr President, we and our free-world partners may soon face the threat of ballistic blackmail.'

For the reasons which I have already mentioned, one should not take as entirely accurate all these somewhat lurid statements. Almost certainly the accuracy of such missiles is likely to be relatively low, so that probably a considerable number of missiles with A-bomb warheads would have to be fired to be sure of knocking out a single base.

Although the early technical possibility of a ballistic missile threat to Western advanced bases has probably been exaggerated, I think that the vulnerability of these bases to medium-range atomic bombers of the Badger class has been under-estimated. At present the main defence against such aircraft is still piloted fighters. These require an exceedingly expensive and complicated radar organization. It is possible, perhaps, that our own and the S.A.C. atomic bases in Britain might be defended for some time, so enabling some effective use of them to be made. But it seems to me unlikely that America could deploy enough day- and night-fighters to protect for long all its advanced bases. Nor could Britain defend our reported atomic base in Cyprus. In a map accompanying a recent article in a British newspaper, this base is shown as allowing British V-bombers to reach far into Central Russia, thus making it a vital threat to the Soviet Union, and so inviting immediate atomic counter-attack with Badgers.

I would therefore reckon that the threat by the Soviet medium-range atomic bombers to the safety of the American and British advanced bases is already rather strong. I am talking here of the direct air threat to the base itself. The indirect threat to the availability of the bases due to the threat to the neighbouring civilian populations (where these exist) is another factor, and at present a much discussed one.

Senator Jackson discusses the political impact of a 1500-mile Soviet ballistic missile on the countries in which S.A.C. bases are, and said, 'It is wellnigh certain that crucial allies would be forced into neutralism, or even into tacit co-operation with Moscow.'

Much prominence to this question of the viability of the key advanced bases has been given in articles, for instance, in the *New York Times*.[11] Three of the most important advanced bases are Thule in Greenland, Keflavik in Iceland and Dahran in Saudi-Arabia. Political changes in Iceland have made it probable that the American armed forces in control of Keflavik may soon have to leave.[12] The agreement to establish the American atomic air base at Dahran comes up for renewal this summer, and the political situation in Saudi-Arabia is now such as to make it possible that this will be refused.

The articles referred to suggest that the loss of these oversea bases would reduce the striking power of the S.A.C. to between one-third and one-fifth of what it is at present. Reliance, then, would be mainly on the B 52 aircraft with an out-and-return operational range of some 3500 miles without refuelling.

If an all-out atomic struggle occurred between America and the U.S.S.R. alone, using only their own continental bases, then there would not be any very marked geographical difference between their offensive and defensive strengths, which would largely depend on their true inter-continental bombers. At present the U.S.S.R. seems to be producing these twice as fast as the U.S.A.

So long, however, as the advanced S.A.C. bases are

operating, it must clearly be a major military aim of Soviet diplomacy, including in this term the use of economic aid, threats, blandishments and political intrigues, to attempt to neutralize them.

In precisely the same way and using the same methods, and for the same *military* reasons—there were other reasons too, of course—the West has attempted to make the Soviets withdraw from the satellite countries to her own ethnic frontiers. For instance, East Germany, Czechoslovakia and Poland are just as important to Soviet defence policy as providing advanced bases from which to threaten Western cities, as are the American and British oversea air bases to Western defence policy. Moreover, these satellite countries also play an important defensive role by allowing a common and extended air defence system.

In the early days of the Western monopoly of atomic weapons, it was the value for air defence of advanced bases in the satellite countries which was important to the U.S.S.R. It is a well-known fact of the bombing offensive of the last War that the losses suffered by an attacking air fleet rose rapidly, in fact much faster than linearly, with the depth of enemy territory into which they penetrated: hence the great importance of depth of defence. Moreover, the faster the attacking planes, the greater the depth of defence required to carry out radar tracking and interception by fighters, and so Russia's still greater need of the satellite countries as advanced bases.

With the growth of the Soviet atomic stockpile, these countries provided advanced bases with an additional offensive role.

Some of these geographical considerations are relevant to the widely-held view that it should be possible to prevent an atomic attack on one's country by destroying the enemy air bases with their aircraft before their attack was launched. Much prominence has been given to the essential importance for Britain to destroy Russian air bases in the first few hours of the war. This is one of the main objectives of the British V-class bombers.

Now undoubtedly such attacks on air bases on both sides would certainly be a feature of the opening stages of a strategic atomic war. Western attacks on the nearer Soviet air bases would be expected and correspondingly Soviet attacks on British and American advanced air bases.

It seems to me exceedingly unlikely that either side would be able to prevent completely by this means an enemy atomic offensive from being launched. For one thing, there are so many possible bases which have to be attacked almost simultaneously at the very outset of a war. Moreover, the now standard air-refuelling technique of bombers allows the aircraft to be operated from main bases very far in the interior of continental land masses and so relatively easy to defend. It has been reported that in an emergency an appreciable fraction of S.A.C. bombers would be kept continuously airborne so as to avoid possible destruction on the ground. The Soviets could do likewise. The headquarters of the American S.A.C. is situated far in the Middle West: no doubt the main Soviet air bases are likewise situated far in the centre of Asia. Forward bases for the refuelling craft would also be required, but any moderate sized airfield could be made use of for this purpose.

So I believe that it would prove technically impossible to implement the policy of destroying Soviet atomic air bases in the first few hours of war. Nor do I think it possible for the U.S.S.R. to destroy all the main Western atomic bases at the outset of a war.

However, suppose that I am wrong and that such an operation is a technically possible one for both sides. Then we get the psychological situation of a duel. The one who strikes first wins; the one who fails to strike first is destroyed. In order not to be destroyed, the West would have to strike first—that is, the West would have to wage what would amount to preventive war. It is, however, almost an article of faith in the West that this cannot be done! Sentiment apart, a loose federation of states as N.A.T.O. is not likely to be good at this type of strategy, which needs strong nerves and quick decisions.

6

The unexpected rapidity with which the Soviet Union has developed atomic weapons and high performance aircraft would alone have suggested a large supply of highly-trained scientists and engineers. In the last few years much detailed study, particularly by de Witt at Harvard,[13] has been made in the West of the Soviet higher educational system, with special reference to the output of scientists and engineers such as are needed for carrying out a modern defence programme. Quite recently, rather startling figures have been given much publicity. Russia is now turning out 60,000 graduate scientists and engineers a year compared with 22,000 in America and some 3000 in Britain. Moreover, the Soviet output is planned to rise at some ten per cent per year. Since 1950 the output of science graduates in Russia has nearly doubled while in America it has fallen to a little over a half. Expressed as the number of engineers per million of the population, the figures today are as follows: U.K. 57, U.S.A. 136, U.S.S.R. 280.

Probably the total number of scientists and engineers in the West is still somewhat larger than in the East, but this will soon be reversed unless the present trend is altered.

It is clear that the present large output of Soviet scientists and technologists is the result of a long-range plan initiated in the middle nineteen-thirties with the avowed object of first equalling and then surpassing the technology of the West. Since, in technology as in war, victory in the long run and on the average goes to the big battalions—of engineers and scientists—the Soviet Union seems likely eventually to achieve her aim if the West does not do something about it.

The difficulty, of course, is that educational advance of a major kind, such as would be required for the West to emulate the East in the output of trained technologists, takes many decades to come to full fruition. The Soviet higher educational plan has been referred to as a fifty-year plan. *The Times* talks of a century's neglect in Britain. Thus no conceivable action in the West could *quickly* reverse the present trend of technological education in favour of the East. One remembers Stephen Leacock's advice to young gardeners: 'Take a garden two years ago.'

Moreover, the type of changes needed are not at all simple nor even primarily financial; on the contrary, they would be of a very deep-seated social kind involving drastic alteration in the traditional concepts of British education. In particular, not only would a larger fraction of an age group have to receive higher education, but a larger proportion of each age group would have to become engineers and scientists at the expense of the arts and humanities. Unless the West is unexpectedly active in the matter of technological education, it is likely to find itself before long technologically inferior to the East, with important consequences in the realm of military strategy.

In Britain, with our small output of scientists and engineers, we are faced with particularly difficult problems—assuming we still aspire to the role of a great power. It is clear that we must use the few scientists we have working on military problems in the most efficient possible manner. This means that it is vital to choose rightly the really important problems in defence technology and not to waste our scientific resources on the less important or the now outdated problems. In fact, we must be exceedingly clever planners in the field of military technology. Now, we can only be clever planners if we face up realistically to the real military situation in the world today. Sloppy and emotional military thinking, based on inadequate historical analysis and fallacious prediction, will surely lead the West into grossly inefficient use of its limited scientific resources.

7

Ever since Hiroshima the West has attempted to assert its world power by reliance on assumed greater resources of science and technology to offset the unwillingness of its citizens to become soldiers.

For it is a matter of willingness and not nearly as much, as is often thought, of numbers of population. When the Second World War ended, America had some twelve million men under arms, which, with some five million in the British and Dominion armed forces, made some seventeen million in all; in comparison Russia had some twelve million men under arms. Moreover, the Western Allies were much stronger in the air and their armies more heavily equipped, particularly as regards mechanized transport.

Immediately after the War the West disarmed very rapidly under the largely fictitious shield of a few dozen atomic bombs. By 1948, the American armed forces numbered 1·5 million and the British 0·75 million. Russia, without atomic bombs herself, and perhaps influenced by the gross exaggeration in the West of the decisiveness of small numbers of bombs in a major war, only reduced her armed services to five million.

By 1947 the reaction against excessive reliance on atomic bombs had begun to set in, and America began to increase her conventional forces. The outbreak of the Korean war further stimulated this rearmament, which had, however, begun before.

The organization in 1948-9 of N.A.T.O. and the plans for twelve German divisions resulted from the waning reliance as a sure defence on the, by then, relatively large stockpile of bombs.

If we now turn to the situation today, we note that, leaving China out of account, Russia and her satellites have a total population of 300 million and maintain 260 active divisions. The N.A.T.O. countries have a population of 230 million in Europe and 400 million in total, but maintain only some twenty active divisions. We have thus deliberately relied on atomic bombs to offset this startling unwillingness of the Western men to become soldiers.

The attempt to meet Soviet armed manpower by atomic weapons led the humane and civilized West to adopt as the mainstay of its military policy the attack on civilians and cities. This 'true use of Air Power'—as it is called by our Air Marshals—is a Western invention, both in theory and in practice: it long pre-dated atomic bombs. The decisive shift in recent months of military opinion away from this doctrine towards the limitation of war, due to the Soviet atomic bombs, has been discussed in detail in the first chapter.

There was one requisite for the former policy to succeed. The West would have had to have made a very determined effort to keep its technological superiority. It did nothing of the sort. What it did do was to relax its efforts generally, except perhaps in the field of atomic weapons, and then was greatly surprised to find its technical lead in military technology threatened. Indeed, the West has been suffering from what has been aptly, if incorrectly, called a 'technological superiority complex'.

I do not think it is generally appreciated to what extent the West has come to believe that its whole survival depends on its military technical superiority; and that if this is lost, defeat or annihilation would follow at once. As the Alsop brothers put it in a recent article in the *New York Herald Tribune*:[14] 'The S.A.C.'s ability to do its grisly job efficiently is quite literally all that prevents the whole world balance of power from tipping decisively in favour of the Communist bloc.'

Senator Jackson put it: 'America's superiority in advanced weapons systems is a *minimum* requirement of peace.' We all remember the talk after Hiroshima of atomic bombs as absolute weapons: the possessor would rule the world. This did not happen. Now it is the I.C.B.M. which is billed as the new absolute weapon. 'Whoever gets there first will have the world by the tail'—these are Bernard Baruch's words.

Let us quote Senator Jackson again: 'Mr President, we have consistently underestimated the Soviets. We underestimated them on the A-bomb: we underestimated them on the H-bomb: we underestimated them on fighter aircraft: we underestimated them on jet bombers. I believe we are now underestimating the Kremlin on ballistic missiles.'

So we now find the West being urged once again to stake its whole survival on winning another technological race. On the other hand, it is clear that very little serious attempt is being made to do so. Faced with this situation it is not surprising to find widespread in the West a mood of deep defeatism. This is markedly in evidence in the 1955 British Defence White Paper, which highlights the choice between subservience to Communism and immense physical devastation of Britain. It cannot but astonish future historians that only a decade has elapsed from 1945 when the West was at the height of its power, to 1955 when such defeatist sentiments could be expressed in an official document.

How much of all this lurid thinking is valid and how much of it is mere declaratory policy masquerading as action policy? Is the situation of the West really as portrayed? I think it will help us to find some kind of answer if we try to study in a little more detail how the present situation has come about. This I will try to do in my last chapter.

CHAPTER III

RETROSPECT AND PROSPECT

1

In the second chapter I described in some detail the intense technological arms race now in progress between East and West, and showed that, though it seems to be the official doctrine that the survival of the Western way of life depends on winning it, no very serious attempts are being made to do so, certainly not in Great Britain.

It is important to note that this doctrine, that a failure in the future to keep a large measure of technological superiority would mean the end of Western civilization, is the obverse of the doctrine that it has been the Western atomic superiority which has saved Western civilization during the last decade. The growth of this concept was clearly a gradual one and grew out of the belief that a relatively few A-bombs would be decisive in a major war, combined with the disinclination of the West to maintain large armies. The doctrine was clearly stated by Mr Winston Churchill in 1948: 'I hope you will give full consideration to my views. I have not always been wrong. Nothing stands between Europe today and complete subjugation to Communist tyranny but the atomic bomb in American possession.'[1]

The difficulty about accepting this proposition is that no one can be foolish enough to believe that, if atomic bombs had not been invented, Western civilization would have collapsed. Suppose that the nuclear fission of uranium had not been discovered until 1948 instead of, as it actually was, in 1938. Would this ten years' delay in a pure scientific discovery really have left the great and mighty West helpless before Communist aggression?

I have already emphasized that, at the end of the Second World War, the armed forces of the Western Allies greatly outnumbered those of the East, and were much more heavily equipped, especially in aircraft and transport: moreover, the West was vastly stronger in industrial capacity. If no atomic bombs had existed, and if a Soviet land attack in Europe had been feared, then the Western Allies would undoubtedly have slowed down their demobilization and kept larger conventional forces in Europe. In the first years after the War, the few atomic bombs in existence were not needed to save Western civilization from Communist aggression.

They did, however, serve to create in 1945 and 1946 an illusion of military strength which seemed to justify a rapid disarmament in conventional armed forces. Belief in this magical theory of defence by a few bombs did not last long.[2] Already by early 1947, when the number of bombs was beginning to rise, the inadequacy of relying on them alone was increasingly realized, and the official campaign in America towards rebuilding Western land forces was well under way three years before the outbreak of the Korean war.

Anyone who believes Churchill's rhetoric about atomic bombs having saved Western civilization must take a much poorer view than I do of the good sense, the high ability, the keen courage and the massive material power of the West. What a pity it is that

Churchill himself did not think of expressing in his unrivalled language the above sentiment!

In retrospect I find it impossible to believe that Western military experts can have thought in the least likely a Soviet land aggression against Western Europe after the War even if no atomic bombs had existed. All the military and material facts were against the possibility. Russia had suffered extremely heavy casualties during the War, at least ten millions compared with the $1 \cdot 6$ million of America and Britain together—out of about the same total population. Moreover, her country had been severely devastated and much of her industry had been destroyed. If she had entertained the idea of conquering Western Europe by force, she would certainly have waited many years to recover from her war injuries and to rebuild her country. The fact that atomic bombs did exist in America and so added an additional deterrence to Soviet aggression, in no way proves that it would have occurred if they had not existed.

Though atomic bombs did not save Western civilization, they had much to do with the course of the Cold War. Here is a field where much detailed historical research is needed before final conclusions can be drawn. The Cold War can conveniently be considered as having started about the time of the Yalta Conference, that is, a few months before the first American bombs were dropped. It appreciably quietened down about the time when both East and West acquired H-bombs. So, historically speaking, the active period of the Cold War nearly coincided in time with the period of Western atomic superiority and so of atomic unbalance. Though clearly serious East-West difficulties would have occurred even if

69

there had been no atomic bombs, I do believe that their existence, and what was said and done about them, greatly intensified them.

How soon the Soviet leaders became aware of the importance of atomic weapons is still unclear, and the various accounts of what President Truman said to Stalin at Potsdam and what Stalin said in reply do not help very greatly. Much depends, of course, on the degree of information the U.S.S.R. acquired from agents during the War of the progress and objectives of the American atomic bomb project. This project started in earnest when General Leslie Groves was put in charge of the Manhattan District—as the project was called—in September 1942. This was during the height of the battle for Stalingrad. In the official report of the Oppenheimer Hearings in 1954, General Groves, when questioned about security matters, said: 'I think it important to state—I think it is well known —that there was never from about two weeks from the time I took charge of the project any illusion on my part but that Russia was the enemy and that the project was conducted on that basis. I didn't go along with the attitude of the country as a whole that Russia was a gallant ally. I always had suspicions and the project was conducted on that basis. Of course, that was reported to the President.'[3]

Possibly, however, it was not till after Hiroshima that Russia decided to go ahead with an atomic programme of her own. How much she was influenced by the early exaggeration of the military decisiveness of the few bombs existing at the time, one cannot tell, but the vociferous clamour of many Western statesmen and journalists may have had an effect. 'The atomic bomb is the Absolute Weapon: all conventional armed forces are out-moded.' 'For the moment, the United States, in terms of power politics, can dominate the world. In comparison Russia is only a vulnerable second-class power.'

Statements like these, even if but partially believed, could only have been taken by Russia as a challenge.

Russia responded to this challenge by building up at high speed her own atomic energy organization, and by speeding up generally her industrial progress on which her military strength depended. Can there be any doubt that Britain, if placed in the same circumstances, would have behaved in the same way?

In addition to the technical and industrial aspects of the atomic arms race there were very important political ones. These were concerned with allies, frontiers and advanced bases. The Soviet Union pressed her military frontiers westward and the West acquired bases round the perimeter of the Soviet Union. Much of the intensity of the Cold War must certainly be attributed to the existence of these geographical aspects of the atomic arms race.

I want now to draw attention to a facet of the atomic arms race which has been many times emphasized, particularly in Britain by Arnold Toynbee.[4] Important aspects of Russian history can be interpreted in terms of a series of attempts to emulate Western technology. Peter the Great's reforms and the introduction into Russia of Western shipbuilding and gun manufacture early in the eighteenth century enabled her to drive out her Swedish invaders. Then a hundred years later came the Napoleonic invasion. Though only achieved with great sacrifice, Russia's final victory proved to herself that she had now matched the power of the West. Then the industrial revolution of the nineteenth century swept over Europe and again left Russia a backward and weak power—as the First World War proved.

As soon as the revolution of 1917 was consolidated, the regime set deliberately about the task of catching up with the West. After making great strides, the Second World War came and inflicted vast damage and loss. But eventually final success came and the German invader was thrown out. At last Russia had come of age technologically, and could expect to be able to relax. Then came the atomic bomb, hailed in the West as the absolute weapon, which relegated the U.S.S.R. to the status of a vulnerable second-class power. The impact of this news on the Soviet Union was certainly very profound. Relaxation was impossible—the technological race had to be run all over again. By a prodigious scientific and industrial sprint the Soviet Union exploded her first atomic bomb only four years behind the now ambling United States, and the first hydrogen test explosion in 1953 less than a year behind. Now we have seen definite signs of relaxation in Russia. But for the atomic bomb and the way it was handled, might not some of this relaxation have occurred in 1945?

2

The explosion in August 1949 of the first Soviet atomic bomb—several years earlier than expected—precipitated in America what has been called 'the fight round the hydrogen bomb'.[5] This culminated, in one aspect, in 1954 with the investigation of the loyalty of J. Robert Oppenheimer and his final dismissal as Adviser

to the Atomic Energy Commission. The 992 unin-
dexed pages of the Hearings will remain for the
historian of our time a unique document. Here we
find high politics and military strategy, nuclear
physics and technology, bitter individual rivalries and
high personal drama. For me, interest is heightened
by my personal friendship with Oppenheimer and
many others among the scientific witnesses, and by my
profound sympathy with them in what must have
been for many an acute personal ordeal.

Of all the fascinating issues raised during the investigation of the loyalty of the man who was most
singly responsible for the rapid development of the
atomic bomb during the War, there are three of outstanding military importance.

The first, and this was the main theme of the controversy of the period 1949–51, was whether the U.S.A.
should attempt a crash programme to make a hydrogen bomb as an answer to the Soviet atomic bomb.

The second subsidiary theme, but a vital one because
of its inter-service aspects, was whether atomic bombs
should mainly be used strategically against cities,
civilian populations and industrial areas, or whether
they should also be used tactically in support of
armies in a land war.

The third was the question of how much national
effort to devote to the air defence of America in comparison with that devoted to the strategic atomic
offensive.

Oppenheimer and many of his scientific colleagues
felt strongly that American military policy had become 'unbalanced' in the sense of concentrating too
exclusively on the strategic atomic offensive to the
neglect both of continental air defence and of the

value of atomic bombs used tactically in land operations. In relation to the latter, the slogan 'bringing the battle back to the battlefield' was used. On both these issues he and his friends fell violently foul of some Air Force circles, and particularly of the Strategic Air Command, who feared that if such policies were adopted, there would be less money and fewer bombs for the S.A.C. The fight, partly in secret and partly in public, was bitter. Oppenheimer undoubtedly showed great moral courage—some have called it foolhardiness—in challenging what has been called the strongest pressure group in Washington, especially in view of his personal vulnerability due to his left-wing past.

It is worth noting that on both the second and third of these issues, those of the tactical use of atomic weapons and of the importance of air defence, Oppenheimer's views subsequently came to be considered as orthodox. He wrote the section of the Vista report which outlined the now accepted Western doctrine of the tactical use of atomic bombs in a land war. He himself took the report to General Eisenhower in Paris, who received it enthusiastically and started to reorganize the defence plans of S.H.A.P.E. accordingly. The problems then raised are still with us and provide one of the main themes of these lectures. There is no doubt that it was this bitter squabble, essentially of a well-known inter-service type, which played a big part in initiating the inquiry into Oppenheimer's 'loyalty'.

The major overt issue of the Hearings in 1954 was, of course, Oppenheimer's initial opposition to the H-bomb programme. This is a most complicated story, but it is so important that I will attempt to give a short, but I hope fair, account of it.

As already emphasized, the Soviet atomic bomb test in August 1949 was a terrific shock to American atomic complacency and stimulated naturally energetic consideration of whether to develop the H-bomb, to reassert American strength and technological superiority. In a very minor way work had been going on ever since 1943 on various aspects of thermo-nuclear or fusion reaction, but on low priority.

Oppenheimer at that time was Chairman of the General Advisory Committee of the Atomic Energy Commission. Other prominent scientific members were James B. Conant, Lee A. Du Bridge, Enrico Fermi, I. I. Rabi, Cyril S. Smith and Glenn T. Seaborg. In addition there were two industrial scientists, Hartly Rowe and Oliver E. Buckley. With the exception of Seaborg, who was abroad at the time, the Committee, though with some qualifications, opposed a large-scale hydrogen bomb programme. Though, no doubt, different individuals gave different weight to the various aspects of the problem, the main grounds for the Committee's opposition in the autumn of 1949 seem to have been as follows: that the H-bomb probably would not work; that it would be extremely expensive in fissile material, which could be used for A-bombs; that it was morally wrong; that if the United States did not make it, the Soviet Union would not be able to; that it was militarily not needed and would lead to a still greater unbalance of America's armed forces; and finally, if both America and Russia had it, that America was more vulnerable.

Early in 1950 President Truman ordered a crash programme to be undertaken.

The H-bomb project which was then thought so

unpromising consisted of a very powerful atomic bomb surrounded by a mixture of deuterium and the fabulously expensive tritium, both probably in a highly compressed or liquified form. This mixture of light elements was to be made to undergo fusion by the heat of the A-bomb. Apparently such a bomb was never made. It was to this project to which Oppenheimer was referring in his letter to J. B. Conant, President of Harvard, when he wrote: 'What concerns me is really not the technical problem. I am not sure the miserable thing will work, nor that it can be gotten to its target except by ox-cart. It seems likely to me even further to worsen the unbalance of our present war plans.'[6]

Then in early 1951 Teller had his bright idea— exactly what it consisted of has never been stated. After this Oppenheimer strongly supported the programme on the explicit grounds 'that it was technically so sweet that we had to have it '.[7]

Part of the explanation of this sudden switch, with its appearance of inconsistency, surprising in one with Oppenheimer's remarkable lucidity of mind, lies, I think, in his explicitly stated belief that the Soviet atomic programme was largely imitative, through publications and agents, of American work. So, at a time when the technical problems to be solved seemed overwhelming even in American eyes, the conclusion followed that if the United States did not, the Soviet Union could not, make an H-bomb. When, however, in the summer of 1951 many of these vast technical difficulties melted away, the argument that the Soviet Union could not make one if the United States did not, melted away also. From what we know now, the scientific advisers certainly exaggerated the degree in which the Soviet atomic programme was imitative. For when the first Soviet fusion test was made in August 1953, it was found to be of a somewhat different type to that tested by America nine months earlier.

An additional factor of importance in changing the scientists' view about the H-bomb was the outbreak of the Korean war in June 1950.

It was only natural and creditable that the scientists who had most to do with developing atomic bombs during the War should be beset by gnawing doubts and, in some cases, intense feelings of guilt about the way they were used. Oppenheimer, above all, with his outstanding achievements in making the bomb possible, certainly was no stranger to these qualms. In a much quoted phrase he wrote: 'In some crude sense, which no vulgarity, no humour, no overstatement can quite extinguish, the physicists have known sin and this is a knowledge they can never lose.'[8] Such feelings were derived from the circumstances of the dropping of the bombs on Hiroshima and Nagasaki, early in August 1945.

Soon after Mr Truman became President, he set up a Committee to advise him on the use of the atomic bombs shortly expected to be available. This Committee, which included Vannevar Bush, K. T. Compton and James B. Conant, with Oppenheimer, Arthur Compton, Ernest Lawrence and Enrico Fermi as advisers, recommended that they be used as soon as possible, without warning against Japanese cities. After the event Oppenheimer admitted a certain consternation at the large numbers of civilians killed in Hiroshima and Nagasaki—about 110,000 in all. The scientists were no doubt at the time consoled by the belief, so authoritatively expressed by President Truman himself, that the dropping of the bombs saved 'untold American lives', sometimes estimated at half a million.[9] This consolation cannot have lasted long, for information gradually became available as to Japan's readiness to surrender well before the bombs were dropped. Certainly by 1947 Oppenheimer was fully aware of the real situation in Japan in the summer of 1945, for he wrote: 'Every American knows that if there is another war, atomic weapons will be used. We know this because in the last war, the two nations which we like to think are the most enlightened and humane in the world used atomic weapons against an enemy which was essentially defeated.'[10]

Then again there is a little-noticed passage in the Hearings. When Oppenheimer was asked when his opposition to the H-bomb started, he replied, 'I think it was when I realized that this country would tend to use any weapon they had.'[11]

Though by 1946, at any rate, it was officially announced that Japan had asked the Soviet Union to negotiate for surrender early in July 1945, there might have been some doubt as to how much of these feelers were passed on to Washington. Recently, however, full details of these negotiations have been published in America in a book by R. J. C. Butow, entitled *Japan's Decision to Surrender*.[12] Butow gives the texts of all the telegrams from Japan's Foreign Minister Tōgō to his Ambassador Satō in Moscow. For instance, about the middle of July, Tōgō cabled to Satō, 'See Molotov before departure for Potsdam. Convey His Majesty's strong desire to secure termination of war. Unconditional surrender is only obstacle to peace.' Satō replied, 'There is no chance whatever of winning Soviet Union to our side. Japan is defeated and must face the fact and act accordingly.' Tōgō then cabled, 'In spite of your views, you are to carry out instructions: endeavour to obtain good offices of Soviet Union in ending the war short of unconditional surrender.'

All these telegrams were decoded at the time in Washington. Of course, there can be no certainty that Japan would in fact have surrendered quickly had no bombs been dropped, but at least—or so any atomic scientists who knew of these cables must have thought—America might have waited some weeks or even months to see. No appreciable loss of American lives would have resulted, as no major military operation against Japan was planned before November.

Once atomic scientists began to doubt the military necessity of the use of the A-bombs on Japan, it was not a long step to begin to fear that the H-bomb, when made, might be used with equally slight military reason. For those atomic scientists who were burdened, in more or less degree, by the guilt of Hiroshima, the thought that they might have a vaster Hiroshima on their conscience cannot have encouraged them to wholehearted support for the H-bomb project. In fact, with few notable exceptions, almost all the scientists concerned opposed the crash programme, at any rate initially. Oppenheimer led this opposition and it was officially, but in fact not only because of this action, that his loyalty was called into question, and his security clearance finally cancelled.

The opposition between 1949 and 1951 of so many atomic scientists to the H-bomb programme must, I think, be taken as the price the American Government paid for lack of candour in 1945. If the scientists had been told that Japan had been essentially defeated and was suing for peace but that the dropping of the bombs won for America a vital diplomatic victory, since it kept the Soviet Union out of the Japanese peace settlement and so avoided the difficulties and frictions inherent in the German surrender, I expect most would have accepted, however reluctantly, the practical wisdom of the act. They were not told this, but they were told that the bomb saved untold American lives. When they later learnt that this was rather unlikely, many of them must have begun to fear that their Government might not be able to resist some future temptation to exploit America's atomic superiority before it was too late.

One outstanding question still remains unanswered. Did the opposition of the scientists between 1949 and 1951 actually delay the H-bomb? No very clear answer emerges from the 992 pages of the Hearings—although this was, of course, a major allegation. On the broader issue as to whether the H-bomb could have been developed earlier, the answer is certainly that it could have been. As far as I know, the final production of H-bombs in 1952–3 depended on no new fundamental scientific discovery—only on brilliant technology and a massive effort. If these had been available in 1945, the H-bomb might have existed in 1949 or even earlier. Possibly it is a good thing for the world that it did not.

Some may consider that there is no sense in now raking over these embers of past controversy and that we should turn our eyes to the future and not to the past. On the contrary, I feel strongly that it is essential to try and understand these events, because of their importance in bringing about the present situation. Here is a case where Descartes's dictum that it is easier to understand something when one watches it grow than when one looks at it fully formed, seems especially valid.

We are not here concerned with any question of right or wrong or even of expediency or inexpediency in the use of atomic bombs on Hiroshima and Nagasaki. Actually, in neither city were more civilians killed than in the great American fire raid on Tokyo in March 1945. Moreover, the total killed was not much more than, say, in the British raids on Hamburg in 1943 and that on Dresden in 1945, taken together.

We are concerned with the consequences of these events. The circumstances of the raids on Tokyo, Hamburg and Dresden fell into the pattern of the then accepted military doctrine, and had few consequences outside the purely military one of contributing to the defeat of the enemy. On the other hand, the circumstances of the case of the first atomic bombs were very special and had, without question, profound effects on the course of post-war history.

Before I leave the discussion of these more subjective and personal matters, I would like to draw attention to two verbal paradoxes, which, though superficial, are, I think, stimulating to thought. Firstly, it is generally believed in the West that it was the American atomic bomb monopoly alone which saved the West from being overrun by the Soviet Union in the years after the War. On the other hand, many now believe that it is the breaking of the American monopoly by the Soviet atomic and hydrogen bombs which has greatly improved the chances of peace. The second and related paradox has a more personal slant. Looked at from the point of view of the individual pioneer atomic scientist of the Los Alamos period, on whose conscience Hiroshima lay heavily, the recent improvement of East-West relations is a vindication of his hope that the horror of the weapon he created would abolish major war. But looked at from the standpoint of the latter-day American and British government atomic scientists, it appears as if it were their failure to maintain the Western atomic lead which has led to the present international détente. Ironical jokes based on this paradox are widely current today in Europe.

Some would perhaps seek to avoid these paradoxes altogether by holding that the improved international relation between East and West is not so much related to the atomic stalemate but is rather a consequence of Stalin's death in March 1953. It would take me too far outside the theme of this book to elucidate this point fully, but there is one obvious military point which must be made.

Though clearly the internal political changes in the U.S.S.R. since Stalin's death have been profound, their fundamental defence policy does not seem to have changed much. With our present knowledge there can be little doubt that for many years past an important element in Stalin's policy was to attempt to impose co-existence on the West by achieving atomic parity. This was, in fact, achieved within six months of Stalin's death—for the first Soviet H-bomb in August 1953 can be considered as signifying the success of the policy.

In so far, then, as the present détente is a result of the present Soviet leaders' confidence in their strength, it is a result not of Stalin's death but of the ruthless methods by which he drove his country to the scientific, technological and industrial efforts, without which atomic parity would have been long delayed.

If the arguments given here are correct, the first proposition of the first paradox—that but for atomic bombs the West would have been overrun by Communism—is untrue. The second proposition—that it is the success of the Soviet atomic programme which has brought a more peaceful atmosphere—requires further analysis, and in particular, a distinction between the effect of the breaking of the American atomic monopoly, on the one hand, and the advent on both sides of H-bombs, on the other. It will be essential here to discuss the rather delicate subject of the theory and practice of preventive war.

3

An essential element in our retrospect of the last decade must be a discussion of the circumstances in which a preventive war is likely to be waged. Now it is a commonplace of the historian of the origin of wars that a danger point is apt to occur when a strong power is faced with the imminent loss of relative power to the growing strength of a rival. Then what seems to the stronger power to be merely a defence of its legitimate interests provides a strong urge to wage preventive war before it is too late.

This situation becomes especially acute in such a period as the present one of rapid technological advance. Dr Cockburn has put it clearly and bluntly. 'In the process of competing for technical or numerical superiority, one side may believe it has achieved a temporary advantage and may embark on a preventive war before the advantage disappears.'[13]

Now, in fact, the objective position of the West in the last decade has been just as described above. The great atomic superiority of America was bound to pass—unless something was done about it. This situation led to much discussion in the U.S.A. of the arguments for and against preventive war. Usually, of course, it was condemned as not a possible policy for the West: but an underlying anxiety is detectable even among its strongest critics, that circumstances might arise which would put power into the hands of its few, but vocal, advocates. Perhaps it was all to the ultimate good that America's atomic monopoly was broken so unexpectedly in 1949: that is, before the strains and exasperations of the Korean and Indo-China wars.

As recently as the spring of 1955 Henry A. Kissinger of Harvard published an article in the *Yale Review* entitled 'American Policy and Preventive War'. He analyses Soviet nuclear progress, their seizing of the initiative in South-East Asia, their alleged capture of the peace offensive and the situation of the West after the collapse of E.D.C. Then comes the following passage: 'Threatened with neutralization or isolation, we are being offered war as a preferable alternative and a preventive war as a means of forcing a showdown before the cards become hopelessly stacked against us.' There follows a reasoned argument against any such attempted solution.

A curious reference to preventive war is found in the Alsop brothers' spirited defence of Oppenheimer in their book *We Accuse*. In order, presumably, to help clear Oppenheimer from any taint of being soft with the Soviets, they wrote: 'Oppenheimer became the only truly eminent American outside the armed forces—so far as these reporters are aware—who was willing to discuss dispassionately the idea of preventive war to save the world from Communist tyranny.'[14]

Any clear-sighted and realistic analysis, from the American point of view, of the strategic situation, say, in 1949 to 1952, must have included a discussion of preventive war. Oppenheimer was certainly clear sighted in these matters, and he probably did fear that some circumstances, perhaps some provocative act of the Soviets, might bring a real danger of preventive war being waged by the West: he may even have toyed with the idea that it might be the right policy for the West.

During the four-year period of atomic monopoly, that is, from 1945 to 1949, America's stockpile was not nearly adequate to defeat the U.S.S.R. in a short and mainly air war. Thus quick and cheap preventive war was not militarily possible during this first period. Moreover, the immediate incentive to it was also not very great, since it was erroneously believed that the U.S.S.R. would not get any bombs till well on in the 1950's.

During the period of quantitative superiority, that is, from the first Soviet A-bomb in 1949 to the first Soviet H-bomb in 1953, both the incentive for and the feasibility of preventive war reached their height. The incentive arose from the rapid atomic progress of the U.S.S.R. and the growing realization in the West of her rapid industrial progress. These, if not checked, might soon neutralize America's atomic superiority, on which the very existence of the Western way of life

depended—so current doctrine alleged. The practicability arose from the now very substantial American
stockpile of ordinary atomic bombs, certainly many
thousands by 1953. These might have conceivably
been adequate to destroy effectively Soviet power
without precipitating a long global land war. I,
myself, do not think so but I admit the possibility.

However, there were two military reasons, in addition to the very strong moral and political ones,
against the West initiating preventive war during this
second period. The first was that, however successful
an atomic attack on Russian cities might prove, it
would not have prevented the Red Army, if it had
wished to, from overrunning Western Europe. Alternatively, the Soviet atomic stockpile, though no doubt
then small, could have inflicted very serious damage on
Western European cities. So, on the whole, Western
military opinion was inevitably very firmly against
preventive war. Moreover, the moral arguments
against preventive war were repeatedly and cogently
argued in the West.

On the other hand, although there were few advocates of preventive war and almost none who would
use the term, there was for a time strong support for
policies which, *if put into practice*, would have
amounted to it. For instance, Mr Winston Churchill
in October 1948 said: 'The Western nations will be
far more likely to reach a lasting settlement, without
bloodshed, if they formulate their just demands while
they have the atomic power and before the Russian
Communists have got it too.'[15] Such a policy could
only be carried out by the clear threat of preventive
war.

In the same year a leader in the London *Observer*

contained the following passage:[16] 'In the wide sphere of diplomacy it is we who hold the trump cards. It is our side not Russia which holds atomic . . . weapons and could, if sufficiently provoked, literally wipe Russia's power and threats from the face of the world.' This last quotation illustrates the profound sense of power engendered by the possession of an atomic monopoly. The belief in absolute atomic power did indeed corrupt judgment.

In the following year or two there was in some circles support for a policy of presenting an ultimatum to Russia as soon as the West was strong enough to do so. As soon, that is, as Western rearmament had proceeded far enough to make it possible to repel the expected Soviet counter-attack by land, the 'year of decision' (as it was sometimes called) would have arrived. Then the West would serve an ultimatum on Russia to retire to her ethnic frontiers and accept the status of a second-class power.

The 'year of decision', originally set for 1952, was gradually postponed as delays occurred in the progress of Western conventional rearmament. After the Soviet H-bomb in August 1953 it was generally but not quite forgotten. For the 'liberation' policy of 1952 to 1953 could only have been implemented by actions which would in effect have amounted to the threat of preventive war. By the middle of 1954 the policy was everywhere recognized as dead.

It is odd to recall that some Western military thinking, particularly centred in Washington, during the critical years 1951 to 1953 assumed that the strength of Russia relative to the West was rapidly deteriorating, so that it was Russia and not the West whose circumstances favoured preventive war. The argument ran that Russia then held a definite military superiority based on land forces throughout the continental landmass of Europe and Asia. It was argued that Western rearmament on land would free the West to use its atomic power and so would end Russia's military superiority. Consequently, it was felt that Russia might accordingly be tempted to wage preventive war. It was further argued that unless she did this, which would mean a suicidal war, she would have to take her place among other powers of the second order, such as Britain, France, Germany, China, India and Japan.

In retrospect it is hard to believe how such a misconception of the real situation can have been seriously entertained. It can only have been based on acceptance of the views of the most extreme advocates of strategic atomic air power. From what we now know of Soviet progress in industrial, military and atomic technology, and of the halting pace of Western rearmament, the Soviet leaders must certainly have believed that time, militarily speaking, was on their side and not on the side of the West. No nation would launch preventive war just before their first H-bomb was completed and when their industrial progress was much faster than that of their opponents, and so rapidly closing the gap between the two sides.

Looking back, then, on this period of military planning, one can view the Western drive to build up its military strength on land to repel a possible Soviet attack as an entirely sensible reaction from the period of undue reliance on atomic weapons. The danger only arose when some political circles thought to use the position of strength so attained not so much to negotiate a settlement as to impose one. Undue hopes began to be entertained as to the positive political successes which would accrue when the position of strength had been attained. It was not always recognized that these political gains could only be achieved by threatening what, in effect, would have amounted to preventive war. However unlikely it was that the West would attempt to impose a settlement of East-West difficulties by force—I think it was always unlikely, except perhaps during a short period in the Korean war—it cannot have appeared certain to the Soviet military authorities, who after all certainly read the Western press and certain speeches of Western statesmen, and who may not always have fully appreciated the declaratory element in them. So one may reasonably conclude that while the chance of the West waging preventive war while it still held a large atomic superiority was always small, it is probable that the fear of the East that the West might do so was real and had much to do with their intransigent policy.

4

Let us now go back to 1946 when the international control of atomic weapons became the dominant diplomatic issue dividing the West and the East. It was early in that year when the famous Acheson-Lilienthal Plan was published by the State Department. This became the basis of the Baruch Plan submitted to the Atomic Energy Commission of U.N.O., where it again formed the basis of the Atomic Energy Commission's own plan, which was subsequently adopted by the Assembly, with only the Soviet powers abstaining.

Now we know more than we did, but not all that we would like to know, of the genesis of these plans. We know that Oppenheimer wrote the Lilienthal Report, or at least claims parentage of all its essential features, including the key idea of combining international control and inspection of atomic energy plants with international ownership.[17] The plan was almost universally acclaimed as a bright ray of hope. It was held that these bold proposals might jerk the world into taking the first steps towards world government.

An important advantage of the plan to the West was that its acceptance by the Soviet Union would force her to lift the Iron Curtain. In the Hearings in 1954, Oppenheimer states that at the time he did not expect the Soviet Union to accept the plan, because he thought that if they did so and opened their frontiers and freely admitted Western inspection, the Soviet system as it existed would collapse.[18] Exactly the same view was expressed to me in New York in 1946 by the late Lord Inverchapel, then the British Ambassador in Washington. I am surprised now, as I was then, that it was considered realistic diplomacy to ask the Soviet Union voluntarily to accept a plan which, in the views of its author and the American and British Governments, would lead to the collapse of the system.

But, in my view, worse folly was to come. When, later in 1946, the Acheson-Lilienthal Plan became metamorphosed into the Baruch Plan, international ownership and inspection was retained and there was added the conception of 'instant and condign punishment' for any transgressions of the control arrangements, to be voted by a veto-less security council, on which Russia was bound to be in a minority.

The story is told that a well-known general who, with Mr Baruch, had been 'putting teeth' into the Lilienthal Plan, said when the final draft was finished, 'Now we have made it so stiff that even the Russians won't be fool enough to fall for it.' Whether true in detail or not, there was certainly a strong military and political group who had no sympathy at all with the high-flown and idealistic phraseology of the Lilienthal-Oppenheimer Plan and publicly campaigned against it. This group was opposed to any international control of atomic energy and preferred an old-fashioned national arms race—which is eventually what came about, since the Atomic Energy Commission plan was rejected by the Soviet Union. The reluctance of Mr Baruch to accept the Lilienthal-Oppenheimer plan as a basis of American policy is shown in his letter to President Truman, quoted in the latter's memoirs.[19]

It is well to remember that Britain in 1946 fully and emphatically supported the thesis that a great power could be quickly and cheaply defeated by atomic bombs alone. The British representative on the Atomic Energy Commission, Sir Alexander Cadogan, said, 'His Majesty's Government fully endorse the emphasis laid in the United States statement on the need for condign, immediate and effective penalties against violation of the future international scheme of control. The greatest deterrent value against any such violation will be the knowledge that punishment will be inevitable and overwhelming.'[20]

Of all the unfortunate aftermaths of this abortive attempt to control atomic energy was the credence it gave to the practicability of waging preventive war against a great power. For this is just what is meant by

91

the infliction of 'instant and condign punishment' by atomic bombs. Perhaps even the Soviet Union fell for this in part—after all they may still have thought themselves ignorant of some essential properties of the weapons. At any rate, they reacted in a perfectly predictable way by energetically starting their own atomic energy programme and making sure that their effective frontiers were pushed as far as possible away from their cities and essential industrial areas to get greater depth of terrain for air defence.

If the Soviet Union had accepted the Atomic Energy Commission plan, she would have been without an indigenous national atomic energy programme, and would have remained technologically inferior in atomic matters. The Prime Minister today justifies Britain's refusal to consider at present the cessation of H-bomb tests by the perfectly correct plea that to do so would leave Britain technologically inferior to America and Russia.

In conclusion I would like to express my own view that U.N.O.'s abortive attempt to control atomic energy in 1946 was disastrous for the immediate interests of the West in the post-war world. The Baruch Plan, with its fatal doctrine of 'instant and condign punishment' against a great power, was the illegitimate offspring of the idealism of conscience-stricken scientists and the conservative realism of hard-bitten statesmen. It was based on the military absurdity that a few dozen atomic bombs could defeat a continental power cheaply and quickly, and so nourished—for many the fear and for a few the hope—of a preventive war. Russia took few real risks in gambling on the chance that the West would not launch one.

The exaggeration of the military decisiveness of a few bombs, on the one hand made the West complacent as to its military and technical superiority and led to the neglect of conventional armaments, and on the other stimulated the East to that additional scientific and industrial effort which enabled it to catch up with the West within a decade. Just as the Soviet A-bomb in 1949 was the immediate cause of a great acceleration of the American atomic programme, so Hiroshima and Nagasaki in 1945 and the doctrine of instant and condign punishment in 1946 must have been the main stimulus to the Soviet programme.

With the advantage of hindsight it could be argued that the position of the West would have been better if no attempt had been made in 1946 to control atomic weapons, that is, if a simple atomic arms race—which is what the military on the whole wanted—had been engaged in from the start. For then there would have been much less reason to exaggerate the power of the bomb and so less justification for neglecting conventional armaments. On the other hand, taking the longer view, the policy that was adopted, by its stimulus to a vigorous Soviet atomic effort, brought forward probably by several years the advent of strategic atomic parity and so the marked reduction of international tension which has gone with it.

I am aware that my views on the early U.N. proposals for the control of atomic energy are not shared by many in the West, and that many even today would echo Mr Ernest Bevin's statement at the General Assembly of U.N.O. in 1948: 'If the black fury and incalculable disaster of atomic war should fall upon us, all I can say is that one Power, by refusing its co-operation in the control and development of these great new forces for the good of mankind, will alone be responsible for the evil which may be visited upon mankind.'[21]

I believe almost the exact contrary: that had the Atomic Energy Commission's plan been accepted by Russia, it would probably have been rejected by America: that if it had been accepted by both, it would not have ushered in a millennium, but might well have led to preventive war being waged by the West. For sooner or later Russia, if she did not collapse as the West hoped, could not have avoided transgressing some edict of the atomic energy authority. Then the Security Council would have been compelled by its instructions to threaten preventive war. Careful reading of the Plan shows that 'instant and condign punishment' was to be meted out, not only against massive aggression but against any substantial infringement of the control arrangement, such as building an unauthorized atomic pile.

It could, of course, be argued that the self-righteousness of Mr Bevin's oratory may have been consciously assumed as a propaganda device. If so, the statement would be assigned to the realm of declaratory rather than action policy, and could well be justified as politically effective. However, one cannot conceal the doubt that Mr Bevin may have been quite sincere in believing in the unqualified moral superiority of the Western attitude to the control of atomic weapons. If so, one could hardly expect much progress in any disarmament negotiations. For just as it is unwise to enter such negotiations with an exaggerated estimate of one's material military strength, so it is equally unwise to exaggerate the strength of one's moral position.

It is, of course, true that 'instant and condign punishment' by atomic attack is a technically feasible operation by the great powers in concert against an errant small power, and may well have a role in some future world order: however just in these circumstances, it might not be required, as other less drastic sanctions would probably suffice. As applied by the West against the East—for this is what the Atomic Energy Commission plan would have entailed—it would have involved U.N.O. in the possibility of legalizing a third world war.

5

This is perhaps a suitable place to return to the prophesies of disaster if the West should ever lose its technical superiority. Firstly, it is clear that the West has already lost much of it and the international atmosphere, far from deteriorating, is definitely improving. At present disaster does not seem imminent. What was the origin of these mistaken predictions?

Clearly the basis of the prediction of disaster if the East should attain technological superiority lay in the assumption that the East would use it as soon as it had it. Basically, the general assumption was that military technological superiority allowed the superior continental power to defeat a weaker continental power quickly and cheaply. If this were so, then it might seem military sense for the Soviet Union to exploit its technological superiority as soon as achieved in this way.

What is clear now is that those in the West who make these prophesies of disaster, are in fact projecting on to the Soviet Union what they thought

American policy was or perhaps should have been. Actually, there is no evidence that I know of, and much to the contrary, that the U.S.S.R. ever thought that a war between continental powers could be anything but long drawn out and fought with all arms. Aerial Blitz Krieg theories, whether with conventional or atomic weapons, have always been derided.

In historic fact such theories are entirely of Western origin. The misunderstood lessons of Pearl Harbour and Hiroshima, reinforced by the 'instant and condign punishment' thesis of the Baruch Plan, led many in the West to think that sudden, devastating and all-out blows were the natural way of waging and winning wars. In fact, the whole vast organization of the American Strategic Air Command was prepared explicitly and only for this type of war. What was more natural than to apply your own theories of war to the enemy! When Senator Jackson says that the West will suffer ballistic blackmail if the East wins the race for the I.C.B.M., then he is, of course, implying that if the West wins the race, then ballistic blackmail *could be* applied to the East. This last proposition is just not true. On the contrary, if the attempt were made to do it, either the bluff would be called or a mutually destructive and probably long drawn out even if broken-backed world war would ensue. In fact, many of the lurid prognostics which are so widespread today in America are the result of attributing to the Soviet Union a Western military theory which they have repeatedly asserted in the past they do not believe and which is certainly now fallacious.

Thus we see that the goal of permanent Western technological superiority is neither attainable nor is it a necessary condition for peace. What is a reasonable and attainable goal is approximate technological parity in certain essential weapons and weapons systems. This would go a long way to ensure that neither side would see any advantage in disturbing the peace. We come back, therefore, very closely to the traditional attitude to military planning, and we can look back on the last decade of technological unbalance as an abnormal one not likely to be repeated.

It would appear that a definite step in this direction is indicated by President Eisenhower's recent comments on the report that the U.S.S.R. has a larger number of long-range atomic bombers than America. He is reported to have stated that it is not necessarily a part of American policy to achieve parity in these aircraft with the U.S.S.R.[22]

So it seems that official Washington opinion is already disposed to ignore the lurid prophesies of disaster, of what would happen if the West lost the lead. Reliance will presumably be increasingly laid— and by both sides—upon the stability resulting from the superiority of offence over defence, rather than the superiority of the offensive power of one side over that of the other. There is, of course, a possible difficulty about any policy which essentially relies on the supremacy of offensive atomic weapons over defensive possibilities. For there is always the conceptual possibility that the balance of destructive offensive power might be upset by a break-through in defence technology. It is an odd situation where a drastic improvement of defence might have highly unsettling effects. However, the technical possibilities of such a break-through seem remote.

Looking back at the last decade, we can see that the attempt to maintain world peace by maintaining permanently Western technological superiority was doomed to failure. It was a dangerous will-o'-the-wisp which might well have enticed the West into waging a preventive war. It is a testimony to the good sense of the West that this did not occur.

6

In this short survey of the events of the first decade of atomic bombs, I have tried to bring out some of the essential steps by which the present situation has come about. In doing so I have felt it necessary to question some deeply-held views, not for the love of criticism for its own sake, but because I am convinced that the only guide to sensible future action is first to understand the past. For all rational action involves an element of prediction, and prediction can only be based on extrapolation from the past. An incorrect description of what has happened may lead to false prediction of what will happen.

There are three main fields where practical decisions have to be taken and they are all closely related.

The first of these is the correct deployment and use of our existing military strength. Now that all-out total war has been made very unlikely by the great superiority on both sides of atomic offensive power over defensive possibilities, I think the major immediate military problems are those relating to small-scale colonial wars such as are in progress now in various parts of the world. A main concern of the Great Powers must be to prevent such wars from starting and if they do start, to prevent them from spreading. It is to the common interest of both East and West to prevent this happening. We already have valuable precedents in the Korean and Indo-China wars to show that this can be done. We all remember the understandable feeling of frustration at the height of the Korean war which led the Americans to feel that never again could they afford another such war. But we can agree much more heartily with the retort that such wars are the only ones that anyone can afford.

Pre-eminent and most tricky is the question as to whether the West can hope to get advantage from the tactical use of atomic weapons to offset its unwillingness to create large armies. I do not know the answer. I believe that the current proposals for such formulae as graduated deterrence and tacit bomb lines, though only first steps, are serious contributions to military thought: after reading the recent Defence debate I think British official opinion is coming slowly and tentatively to think so too but is too timid to say so clearly. If, however, they and other analogous proposals to make a distinction between strategical and tactical atomic weapons do prove impracticable, then I am convinced that the alternative is not to return to massive atomic retaliation against cities, except in a situation where a nation is prepared to commit suicide to avoid defeat, but to use no atomic bombs at all—not even on the battlefield.

It is an old crack, however unjust, that the natural conservatism of soldiers makes them plan the next war with the concepts of the last war but one. It seems to me that, historically speaking, the extreme advocates of air power have often planned on the basis of the next war but one. The early enthusiasts before the First World War assumed an air potential that did not mature till late in the Second World War. The Douhets and Mitchells of the nineteen-twenties assumed an air destructive power which only became actual with large stockpiles of atomic bombs about 1949. Today strategical atomic weapons have not only cancelled themselves out and so made all-out total war exceedingly unlikely, but have finally abolished the possibility of victory by air power alone against a great power. Thus much future military planning will inevitably be concerned with wars fought with more limited weapons and for more limited objectives than World War II. So perhaps now the soldiers really should plan for the last war but one.

The second field for decision is the development of future weapons. What types of weapon should we make: what aircraft, atomic bombs, long-range rockets, and defensive guided missiles should be produced?

I think we should act as if atomic and hydrogen bombs have abolished total war and concentrate our efforts on working out how few atomic bombs and their carriers are required to keep it abolished. In the next few years I see the problem not as how many atomic bombs we can afford but as how few we need. For every hundred million pounds spent on offensive and defensive preparations for global war, which almost certainly will not happen, is so much less for limited and colonial wars, which well may.

In our present struggle both to retain our traditional power, for instance, in the Middle East and to maintain peace there and elsewhere, it is troops, guns, tanks, air and land transport and tactical air power that we are desperately in need of—not atomic bombers or the active defence systems against them. As already mentioned, the *local* effect of Britain's atomic bombers on the balance of power in these areas may well be negative: for the demonstration of British air power may be more than cancelled out by fear of the result of giving base facilities for it to be used.

It is very generally agreed now that a direct result of the atomic strategic stalemate is increasingly to switch the Cold War to retaining or winning the allegiance of the uncommitted and under-developed areas of the world. This is the arms-race-into-aid-and-trade race theme. To run an aid-race much money is wanted, and the only source which would not check the rise of our Western living standards would be by reducing our total arms budget. To run a trade-race requires much of our scientific resources switched from arms to the export industries.

The third field for decision lies in the problems of international control of atomic weapons and of general disarmament. The fact that I have said so little about this problem does not mean that I do not think it of the highest importance: it does mean that I am convinced that real progress towards disarmament can only come from a realistic appreciation of the global military situation. Each country's proposals for atomic disarmament and control will inevitably be based on its own views of the role of atomic weapons in the types of wars which it can envisage itself as fighting.

During the period of American atomic monopoly the short-range interests of America and Russia were inevitably poles apart. This is the essential cause of the failure of all the early attempts at atomic control. Now with the period of atomic parity approaching, the interests of West and East are coming much closer.

There is a marked quietening of the tone of the discussions on atomic control going on today between East and West compared with those of the early period in 1946–8. One has only to compare both the content and style of the recent Eisenhower-Bulganin exchange of letters with many of the corresponding exchanges of ten years ago.

I do not think it is useful to go further than to emphasize the improvement in atmosphere resulting essentially from the increasingly similar interests of East and West. The particular proposals from both sides now under discussion are inevitably to some extent declaratory in content. On what terms both sides would be prepared to settle, I doubt if they yet know themselves. Clearly much hard bargaining is in store, but now it is bargaining between effective atomic equals, and this gives much greater hope for agreement: one should not take too seriously the absurdities of the game of musical chairs now being played at the disarmament conference at St James's.

Though at present the outlook for a disarmament *agreement* looks black, the outlook for actual disarmament looks good. For we seem to be moving into a period of what may be called competitive unilateral disarmament. The U.S.S.R. has recently made a politically clever move and now it is the West's turn to play, if only for economic reasons.

This is where the need for a sound and accepted body of military doctrine becomes vital: without it there is no way of assessing the value of the different components of our defence system and so of estimating what parts can most easily be dispensed with, and

102

what parts perhaps should be strengthened. The arguments and analyses of this book, incomplete and tentative as they are, are intended as a contribution to working out a rational defence policy in a world in which atomic and technological parity between the two main contending power groups is the only permissible assumption for planning purposes.

I do not, however, expect soon any startling outcome or final solution. Gradualness is here, I am convinced, inevitable. We have to learn to live with bombs, as we are indeed doing every year, and every year we live with them without using them is one step towards the possibility of a real agreement on how first to control them and how then to abolish them.

REFERENCES

CHAPTER I

1. A. Toynbee, *Civilization on Trial* (O.U.P. 1948), p.166; *The World and the West* (O.U.P. 1913), p. 7.
2. F. O. Miksche, *Atomic Weapons and Armies* (Faber, London, 1955); G. C. Reinhardt and W. R. Kintner, *Atomic Weapons in Land Combat* (Military Science Publishing Co., Harrisburg, Penn. U.S.A.).
3. A. Buzzard, *International Affairs*, 32 (1953), p. 148. *Manchester Guardian*, 31 October 1955; *Spectator*, 9 March 1956.
4. J. Slessor, *International Affairs*, 32 (1956), p. 158.
5. R. Cockburn, *Journal, Royal United Services Institution*, 30 November 1955.
6. B. L. Montgomery, *Journal, Royal United Services Institution*, November 1954, p. 507.
7. B. L. Montgomery, *Journal, Royal United Services Institution*, November 1955, p. 509.
8. B. L. Montgomery, Press Conference at Annual N.A.T.O. Exercise, quoted in *Manchester Guardian*, 28 April 1956.
9. M. B. Ridgway, *Saturday Evening Post*, 22 January 1956.
10. L. Szilard, *Bulletin Atomic Scientists*, October 1955.
11. J. F. Dulles, Speech, 8 December 1955.
12. *Statement on Defence*, 1956 (H.M. Stationery Office), p. 23.
13. *Ibid.* p. 4.
14. T. H. Finletter, *Power and Policy* (Harcourt Brace, New York, 1954), pp. 144–8.
15. *Life International*, 20 February 1956.

CHAPTER II

1. Scientific Correspondent of *Manchester Guardian*, 27 February 1956.
2. *Ibid.*

3. *New York Times*, quoted by *Manchester Guardian*, 13 June 1955.
4. H. Hart, *Bulletin Atomic Scientists*, June 1954.
5. *U.S. Strategic Bombing Survey*, quoted by Blackett, *Military and Economic Consequences of Atomic Energy* (London, 1948).
6. Mr Quarles, quoted by *The Times*, 16 March 1956.
7. President Eisenhower, quoted by *Manchester Guardian*, 10 March 1956.
8. Senator H. N. Jackson, excerpt from speech in *New York Times*, 2 February 1956.
9. J. and S. Alsop, *New York Herald Tribune*, 4 December 1955.
10. A Hetherington in *Reporter* (New York), 14 March 1955.
11. H. Baldwin, *New York Times*, 5 February 1956.
12. *Manchester Guardian*, 29 March 1956.
13. N. de Witt, *Soviet Professional Manpower*, 1955; *Technical Education* (H.M. Stationery Office, February 1956), Appendix A.
14. J. and S. Alsop, *New York Herald Tribune*, 4 December 1955.

CHAPTER III

1. *Europe Unite.* Mr Winston Churchill's speeches (London, 1950), p. 413.
2. J. and S. Alsop, *We Accuse* (London, 1955), p. 42.
3. *In the Matter of J. Robert Oppenheimer* (U.S. Government Printing Office, Washington, 1954), p. 173.
4. A. Toynbee, *loc. cit.*
5. J. Shepley and C. Blair, *The Hydrogen Bomb* (New York, 1954); J. and S. Alsop, *loc. cit.*
6. *Oppenheimer Hearings*, *loc. cit.* p. 242.
7. *Ibid.*; see also p. 251.
8. Shepley and Blair, *loc. cit.* p. 48.
9. H. S. Truman, *Year of Decision* (London, 1955), p. 347.

REFERENCES

10. J. R. Oppenheimer, quoted by Blackett, *loc. cit.* p. 178.
11. *Oppenheimer Hearings*, p. 250.
12. Robert J. C. Butow, *Japan's Decision to Surrender* (Stanford University Press and O.U.P., 1954).
13. R. Cockburn, *loc. cit.*
14. J. and S. Alsop, *loc. cit.*
15. Winston Churchill, *loc. cit.* p. 414.
16. *Observer*, 27 June 1948.
17. *Oppenheimer Hearings*, p. 38.
18. *Ibid.*
19. H. S. Truman, *Years of Trial and Hope* (London, 1956), pp. 9 ff.
20. A. Cadogan, quoted by Blackett, *loc. cit.* p. 135.
21. E. Bevin, quoted by K. Ingram, *History of the Cold War* (London, 1955), p. 124.
22. President Eisenhower, *loc. cit.*